D0754392

EGYPT
in Pictures

VGS

Jeffrey Zuehlke

WITHDRAWN

Contents

Website address: www.lernerbooks.co

Lerner Publications Company
A division of Lerner Publishing Group
241 First Avenue North
Minneapolis, MN 55401 U.S.A.

web enhanced @ www.vgsbooks.com

Library of Congress Cataloging-in-Publication Data

Zuehlke, Jeffrey, 1968–
    Egypt in pictures / by Jeffrey Zuehlke—Rev. & expanded.
      p.   cm. — (Visual geography series)
    Includes bibliographical references and index.
    Summary: Discusses the physical features, history, government, people, culture, and economy of Egypt.
    ISBN: 0-8225-0367-0 (lib. bdg : alk. paper)
    1. Egypt—Juvenile literature. 2. Egypt—Pictorial works—Juvenile literature. [1. Egypt.] I. Title. II.
Visual geography series (Minneapolis, Minn.)
DT49 .Z84 2003
962—dc21   2001006613

Manufactured in the United States of America
1 2 3 4 5 6 — JR — 08 07 06 05 04 03

INTRODUCTION

When discussing Egypt and its history, one inevitably speaks in terms of thousands, not hundreds, of years. The country's rich history spans more than five millenia. Egypt's longevity as an important strategic entity rests on two key factors: Positioned on the northeastern corner of the African continent, Egypt has served as a hub for commerce between Africa, the Mediterranean region, and Asia for thousands of years. Secondly, the country's Nile Valley is one of the world's most fertile agricultural regions, serving as a major grain producer since ancient times.

In ancient times, Egypt was characterized by thousands of years of self-rule, creating stability that allowed great advances in urban life, agriculture, written communication, mathematics, and architecture. For much of the past two millenia, Egypt's strategic position and agricultural resources made the country a target for expanding empires. Egypt's long period of domination by foreign powers began in 332 B.C., when Greek conqueror Alexander the Great added the country to his empire. Outsiders—the Romans, Arabs, Ottomans, and British in

succession—continued to dominate Egypt until the country finally regained its full independence in 1956.

Since becoming an independent nation, Egypt has struggled to grow as a modern state and as a leader of the Arab world. In the 1950s and 1960s, the Egyptian government, led by President Gamal Abdel Nasser, instituted socialist economic policies and sought economic and military aid from the Soviet Union. But socialism failed to cure Egypt's economic problems. In the 1970s, the Egyptian government turned to a capitalist approach and looked to the West for political and economic support.

Present-day Egypt faces many challenges. Official population estimates for Cairo, the capital of Egypt and the largest city in Africa, are 6.8 million, but unofficial estimates are more than twice as high. The overcrowding of this city, as well as the overall rise in the country's population, has created serious problems in housing, employment, sanitation, and transportation.

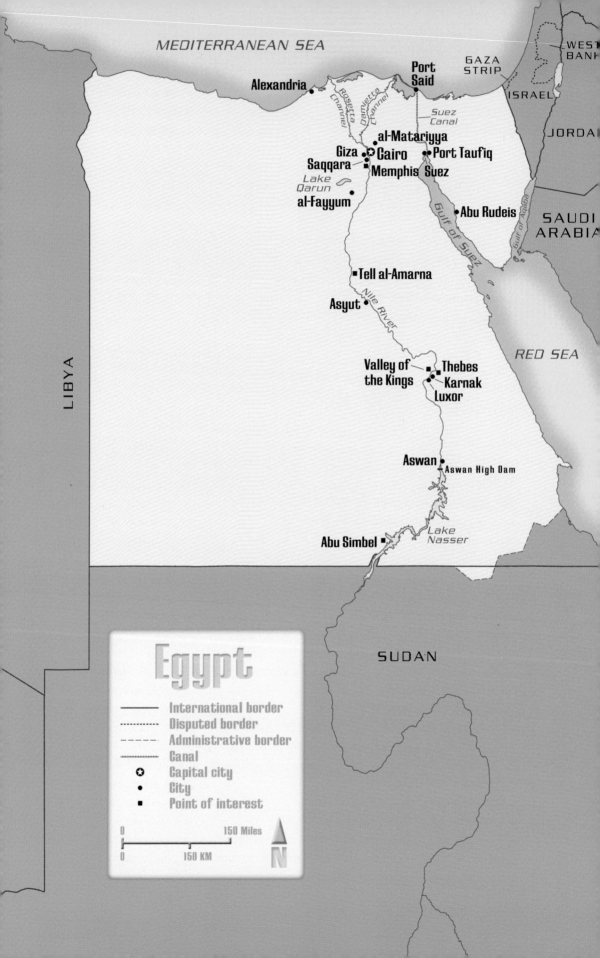

Overpopulation is not Egypt's only challenge. As an Arab nation, Egypt has had a history of warfare with Israel, a nation formed in 1948 to create a homeland for the Jewish people. In 1979, however, Egypt became the first Arab state to make peace with Israel. This action created tension between Egypt and its Arab neighbors—as well as among its own people—many of whom opposed reconciliation with Israel. Relations between Egypt and Israel have been strained in the 2000s, as Egyptians have been critical of Israel's strong military responses to Palestinian uprisings in the West Bank and Gaza.

Egypt also faces internal political challenges from Islamic fundamentalist groups whose goal is to overthrow the country's secular (nonreligious) leadership. Violent acts on the part of the fundamentalists have resulted in crackdowns by the Egyptian government. This struggle between secular and sectarian (religious) forces, in addition to a struggling economy, have combined to create political and social challenges for the nation's leaders.

Terrorist attacks on the United States by Islamic militants on September 11, 2001, impacted Egypt both politically and economically. The Egyptian government immediately condemned the attacks and offered intelligence support to the United States in the resulting war against terrorism. The terrorist attacks were allegedly the work of an Afghanistan-based militant Islamic group known as al-Qaeda, many of whose leaders are Egyptian exiles. The Egyptian government increased its suppression of Islamic militants and suspected terrorists in the wake of the attacks. The terrorist acts had a devastating effect on Egypt's economy. Fears of further terrorist attacks left many potential tourists reluctant to travel, crippling Egypt's tourism industry. These events added further pressure to Egypt's economy, which was in the middle of a deep recession at the time, increasing the challenges that face the nation as it moves into the twenty-first century.

THE LAND

Egypt lies in the northeastern corner of Africa at the point where the African and the Asian continents meet. The Mediterranean and Red Seas form natural water boundaries on the north and east, respectively, and straight cartographic lines determine Egypt's western border with Libya and its southern boundary with Sudan. These boundaries are not accidental. Although Egypt has a long history, its present size was determined mainly by the British during the colonial period, which lasted from the 1880s until the 1920s.

Egypt has an area of 386,660 square miles (1,001,445 square kilometers)—about equal in size to the states of Texas and California combined. While the country is large, only about 4 percent of its land is suitable for farming—a fact that has dominated life in Egypt for centuries. A narrow strip of fertile territory lies along the Nile River, stretching north from Aswan and including the Nile Delta. Ninety-five percent of the population lives near the banks of the Nile. The rest of the country is desert, although the Egyptian government has several

major engineering projects under way to reclaim millions of acres of desert land for farming.

The country can be divided into four main regions. The Nile Delta and Valley cut through the country's eastern edge. The Western Desert and Eastern Desert comprise its midsection, and the Sinai Peninsula forms Egypt's northeastern corner.

◎ The Nile River and Delta

Beginning in Tanzania, the Nile River flows northward through Uganda, Sudan, and Egypt and empties into the Mediterranean Sea. In Egypt the Nile Valley is a green strip 10 miles (16 km) across at its widest point before it reaches Cairo, where it widens into the fields and sandbars of the delta. In this triangular region at the mouth of the Nile, the waterway splits into several channels. Its two main channels are the Damietta and the Rosetta, named for the cities at their mouths. The delta is 100 miles (160 km) long and, at the Mediterranean coast, 155 miles (249 km) wide.

Forming a fertile valley that runs the length of Egypt, **the Nile River** has been a lifeline for farmers, merchants, and travelers for thousands of years.

Four shallow, salty lakes extend along the delta's Mediterranean border.

Almost all of Egypt's farmland lies along a 960-mile (1,545-km) stretch of the Nile. South of Cairo, the Nile Valley is lined with cliffs of granite, sandstone, and limestone. For centuries this portion of the valley has been referred to as Upper Egypt, and the delta has been known as Lower Egypt. The southernmost section of the Nile Valley is part of a region called Nubia, which extends southward from the city of Aswan far into Sudan.

⊙ Deserts

The Western, or Libyan, Desert is part of the great Sahara Desert, which covers about two-thirds of Egypt and averages 600 feet (183 meters) above sea level. Some highlands, however, such as the Jilf al-Kabir Plateau, rise to 3,000 feet (914 m). The Western Desert has vast hollows, including the Qattara Depression, which at 440 feet (134 m) below sea level is the lowest point in Africa. A lake, Birket (Lake) Qarun, fills another depression north of the town of al-Fayyum. A huge, sandy area within the Western Desert is referred to as the Great Sand Sea.

The Eastern Desert, often called the Arabian Desert, is also part of the Sahara and extends eastward from the Nile. Separated from the

Nile Valley by sharp cliffs, the Eastern Desert rises gradually, with some jagged, volcanic mountain peaks over 7,000 feet (2,134 m) high along the Red Sea. Dry riverbeds, called wadis, cut deep channels across the Eastern Desert, giving it a very irregular surface. Occasionally during winter rains, water flows through these wadis. The southern edge of this region is known as the Nubian Desert and extends into Sudan.

The Sinai Peninsula is separated from the rest of Egypt by the Gulf of Suez—which is an arm of the Red Sea—and by the Suez Canal. The peninsula is flanked by the Gulf of Aqaba, which is another extension of the Red Sea, and by Israel on the east. Geographically, the Sinai Peninsula is part of southwestern Asia.

A flat, sandy desert in the north, the Sinai Peninsula consists of mountainous desert in the south and contains Egypt's highest peak, Mount Catherine (8,652 feet/2,637 m). Nearby, rising 7,497 feet (2,285 m) above sea level, stands Gebel Musa, or Mount Sinai. Many believe this is the Mount Sinai on which, according to the Bible's Old Testament, Moses received the Ten Commandments.

The Aswan High Dam

In 1971 the Aswan High Dam was completed to control flooding of the Nile River. The backed-up waters of the Nile formed Lake Nasser, which stretches 150 miles (241 km) south and reaches into Sudan. Some experts believe that the dam saved Egypt from the famine that ravaged eastern Africa, especially Ethiopia, during 1985 and 1986. An additional benefit from the dam is the quantity of electricity generated by its hydroelectric plant.

Although it has been successful in increasing arable land and providing electricity to a large part of Egypt, the Aswan High Dam has also caused environmental problems. Its control of the flow of the Nile has eliminated the annual flooding that brought with it a rich silt. Before the dam became operational, farmers depended on this silt to

---

SAHARA FACTS

The Sahara Desert is the largest desert in the world, covering nearly 3.5 million square miles (9 million sq. km). It extends across nearly the entire northern one-third of the African continent, from the Atlantic coast to the Red Sea. The desert's name comes from the Arabic word for desert, *sahra'*. The Sahara Desert's average annual rainfall is less than 4 inches (10 centimeters). The highest official temperature ever recorded on earth was in the Sahara Desert—136°F (58°C) at al-Aziziyah, Libya.

The Aswan High Dam is built almost entirely of local Aswan granite. The dam benefits Egypt by controlling the annual floods on the Nile.

keep their soil fertile. Because of this change, Egyptian farmers have been forced to turn to chemical fertilizers, which are expensive and place additional strain on the environment. The loss of silt has also increased erosion in the Nile Delta.

In 1997 Egyptian workers began excavations for a canal that will carry water pumped from Lake Nasser through the Western Desert. Planners hope that the New Valley Canal project will turn barren desert into farmland by providing water for irrigation.

Climate

Egypt has a dry climate throughout the year, with a hot season from May to September and a cool season from November to March. The country depends almost entirely on water from the Nile River and from wells. Even the Mediterranean coast, where the most rain falls, averages only 8 inches (20 centimeters) of precipitation a year. Cairo receives only about 1 inch (2.5 cm) of rain per year, and many Egyptians who live in the southern part of the country have never seen rain.

During the summer, the temperature in the desert at noon may exceed 110°F (43°C). But the temperature drops sharply after sunset, so evenings are cool. Cooling winds that blow from the Mediterranean Sea moderate average summer temperatures near the coast. In this area, temperatures range from 80° to 90°F (27° to 32°C). The winters are mild with clear sunny days and cool nights. Winter temperatures range from 55° to 70°F (13° to 21°C). Desert temperatures, however, can be much colder during the winter.

Hot, dry desert winds called *khamsin* occasionally blow in from the Sahara, bringing with them an extreme rise in temperatures and low humidity. These storms carry dust and sand and can damage crops.

◉ Flora and Fauna

Because of Egypt's dry climate, vegetation is confined largely to the Nile Valley, the delta, and desert oases (fertile areas). The most common native tree is the date palm. Other trees include the sycamore, acacia, and carob. Eucalyptus and various fruit-bearing trees have been introduced from foreign countries. In the rich soil of the delta, grapes, vegetables, and flowers— such as lotuses, jasmines, and roses— thrive. In the desert, alfa grass and several kinds of thorn plants can be found.

Date palms

Although papyrus once grew all along the Nile and was harvested for making paper, in modern times it grows only in southernmost Egypt.

Snakes that are native to Egypt include the poisonous Egyptian cobra and the horned viper. Lizards are numerous. Although the hippopotamus and crocodile were common in both Upper and Lower Egypt during ancient times, in modern times they are confined to Upper Egypt.

The Egyptian cobra, or asp, is a venomous snake. The figure of an upright cobra adorned the crowns of ancient Egyptian rulers. The snake was believed to protect the king or queen and was considered an agent of the ruler's destructive powers. To see pictures and to learn more about the wildlife native to Egypt, visit vgsbooks.com for links.

Gazelles inhabit the desert, and hyenas, foxes, jackals, wild asses, boars, mongooses, and jerboas (a type of rodent) roam the Nile Delta and the mountains along the Red Sea.

Bird life is abundant in Egypt, especially in the delta and valley of the Nile. About three hundred species of birds—including sunbirds, golden orioles, egrets, pelicans, flamingos, herons, storks, and quail—exist in the country. Birds of prey include eagles, falcons, vultures, owls, and hawks. More than one hundred species of fish live in the Nile and in the lakes of the delta, providing sport and livelihood for anglers.

◑ Natural Resources

The cliffs bordering the Nile are composed largely of limestone and sandstone. Harder stones—such as granite, alabaster, and quartzite—are found in the river area. Some deposits of iron ore, phosphate rock, and gold also exist.

During the 1970s, the Israelis—who controlled the Sinai Peninsula after the Six-Day War in 1967—expanded and developed oil fields at Abu Rudeis and in the Gulf of Suez. When Egypt regained the region in 1975, it took over the oil fields. At the beginning of the twenty-first century, oil accounted for nearly 36 percent of Egypt's exports.

◑ Cairo

Current estimates indicate that as many as 16 million people live in Egypt's capital city of Cairo. Unemployment in rural areas has led millions of Egyptians to move to the capital in search of work. This

With a population estimated at 16 million, **Cairo** is one of the world's most crowded cities. For a link to the most up-to-date population figures for Cairo, go to vgsbooks.com.

One of the best places to experience the hustle and bustle of Cairene life is at **the Khan al-Khalili bazaar.**

mass exodus has resulted in an intensely overcrowded city, where modernization has not kept pace with the demands of the huge population. Some neighborhoods in Cairo contain two million people. In poor parts of the city, hundreds of thousands of people live in impoverished conditions with no plumbing or electricity.

Cairo is a place where ancient and modern ways mingle. Interspersed with trucks and automobiles are donkey carts and camels. Businesspeople dressed in European clothing walk alongside Egyptians wearing the long, flowing robes that have been common for centuries.

The hub of Egyptian industry and government, Cairo is also a center of culture and of Islamic religious study in the Arab world. Members of Egypt's middle class live in high-rise housing and shop at modern stores. Beside these modern structures stand bazaars (street markets), an ages-old commercial forum, where goods are sold by bargaining and where strict Islamic religious ways persist. Around the Khan al-Khalili bazaar, for example, women often wear veils in observance of traditional Islamic codes of modesty.

Port Cities

Alexandria—the second largest city in Egypt, with a population of more than 3.3 million people—is situated on the north coast, near the western mouth of the Nile. In ancient times, Alexandria was the great-est commercial city of the Mediterranean world and a focal point of learning. The city still serves as the chief port of Egypt. Alexandria—

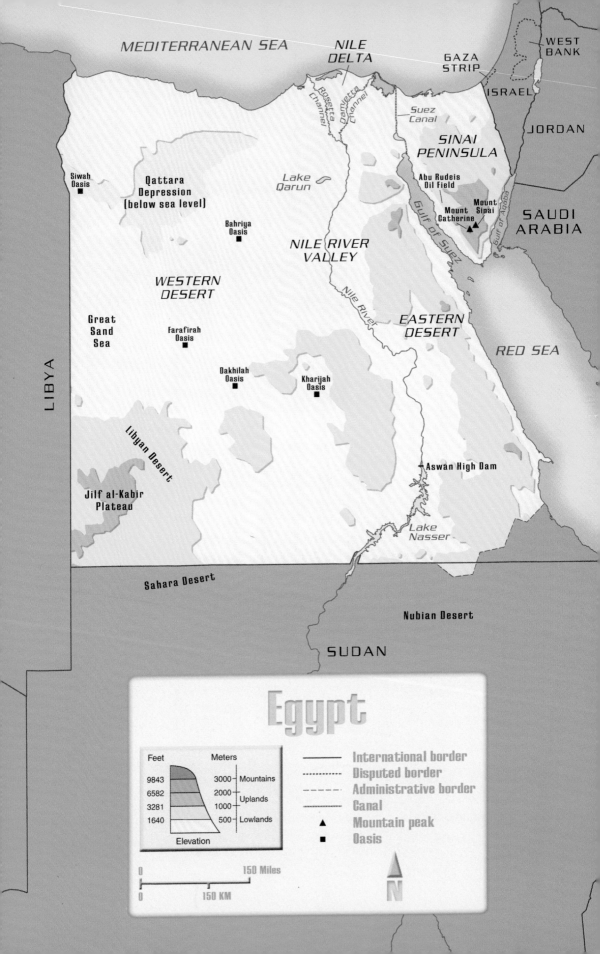

where Cleopatra once reigned as queen—is an attractive, modern city with many academic institutions, parks, cafés, and marble monuments. Alexandria hopes to recapture its former status as an intellectual center with the construction of a giant new library that will house a huge collection of both ancient and modern materials.

> If you'd like to learn more about both the ancient and new Alexandria libraries, visit vgsbooks.com for a link where you can find current information about the new library and several articles about the ancient library and the scholars who studied there.

Port Said (population 472,000) is located at the Mediterranean entrance to the Suez Canal. Founded in 1859—the same year construction of the canal began—much of the city is an artificial island made with sand from the canal's excavation. Port Said is a popular resort town among Egyptians, in part because the port does not charge taxes on imports.

This passenger ferry shuttles people from Port Said to al-Matariyya.

Suez (population 418,000) lies at the southern entrance to the Suez Canal, overlooked by the peaks of the Sinai Peninsula. New deposits of oil have been discovered south of Suez, and the city has a large oil refinery. Neighboring Port Taufiq stands on an artificial island connected to Suez by a causeway (a raised road across wet ground or water).

Secondary Cities

About 90 miles (145 km) southwest of Cairo by rail lies al-Fayyum (population 212,000), the largest natural oasis in Egypt. Waterwheels and water-powered mills abound in al-Fayyum, where small streams and springs irrigate vineyards and citrus groves.

Asyut (population 321,000) is one of the most important provincial, commercial, and educational hubs in Egypt. For centuries, caravans visited Asyut from the interior of Africa, especially from Sudan, bringing trade items to Egypt. Asyut is one of the most modern communities in

Egypt, with a high standard of education and its own university.

Farther south along the course of the Nile in Upper Egypt lies Luxor (population 138,000), a resort town with several ancient ruins. Nearby is the site of Thebes, which was once the capital of the pharaohs (Egyptian rulers). Along the east bank of the Nile is the Temple of Amen (the Egyptian king of the gods) at Karnak, and on the western bank lie the Valley of the Kings, the Valley of the Queens, and the Tombs of the Nobles, where the treasures of Tutankhamen were discovered in 1922.

Aswan (population 220,000) stands at the edge of Nubia in southern Egypt and is surrounded by desert. The massive Aswan High Dam adds to the city's importance. Aswan has ancient origins as a frontier town, but its present prosperity dates from the original Aswan Dam, built by the British in 1902. A new fertilizer plant has also boosted the economy of Aswan, and more development is planned.

Al-Fayyum is home to an oasis that creates a rich pocket of farmland in Egypt's arid landscape.

HISTORY AND GOVERNMENT

Archaeological discoveries of ancient villages and cemeteries in Egypt have revealed that, long before recorded history, people from other parts of Africa and from western Asia cleared and settled the swamps of the Nile Valley. These people cultivated crops, raised livestock, developed art forms, and conducted trade.

About 3100 B.C., an Egyptian king, often referred to as Menes, united the country from north to south and made Memphis (near present-day Cairo) the capital. Menes was the founder of the first dynasty (ruling family) of Egypt and was also the first of many pharaohs (kings). The thirty dynasties that followed have been grouped into Old, Middle, and New Kingdoms, with intermediate periods between each kingdom.

During the first two dynasties, sometimes called the Archaic Period, Egyptians began to use hieroglyphics, a form of picture writing. They also built huge tombs, called mastabas, which evolved into the pyramids of later periods. The ancient Egyptians believed in life after

death, and they entombed their dead with provisions for existence in the afterlife. The elaborate tombs contained large rooms packed with furniture, tools, hunting weapons, food, and drink for the deceased to use in the next world.

The Old and Middle Kingdoms

Pyramids appeared during the third dynasty, which began around 2700 B.C. Each king from the next several dynasties built his own massive tomb. Slave laborers designed and constructed twenty large pyramids. The three most impressive structures were built at Giza, near present-day Cairo, for the pharaohs Khufu, Khafre, and Menkure.

The pharaohs of this period were absolute rulers who were considered gods on earth, and their civilization was highly developed. The Egyptians were advanced in all the arts and sciences. For example, their remarkable knowledge of geometry is demonstrated by the precision of their architecture.

From 2200 to 2050 B.C., Egypt fell into the turmoil of the First Intermediate Period. Warring families tried to gain the throne, and pharaohs no longer held supreme authority. The strife forced a decline in commerce and the arts as the unity of Upper and Lower Egypt crumbled. Regional officials, called *nomarchs,* became powerful.

Mentuhotep II, the last ruler of the eleventh dynasty, reunified Upper and Lower Egypt during his reign from 2060 to 2010 B.C., which signaled the beginning of the Middle Kingdom (2050–1650 B.C.). Despite occasional rebellions, Mentuhotep restored the central power of the throne and established his capital at Thebes (present-day Luxor).

Statue of Mentuhotep

The pharaohs of the twelfth dynasty showed not only strength but compassion as well, promoting an image of themselves as "good shepherds" rather than remote gods. Amenemhet I and his successors increased Egypt's wealth and power. Military forces conquered Nubia to the south, and Egyptians traded with Palestine and Syria in southwestern Asia. Architecture, literature, and other art forms also flourished during this period.

In the Second Intermediate Period (1650 to 1550 B.C.), the dynastic rulers again weakened. Eventually, Egypt was overpowered by the Hyksos, invaders from western Asia. The Hyksos used new technologies that included horses, chariots, armor, and superior weapons to subdue and dominate the Egyptians.

The ancient Egyptians believed in life after death, and that a deceased person's body required preservation for this new life. Because of this, the ancient Egyptians developed sophisticated techniques of mummification. The process included removal of most of the body's internal organs, filling the abdomen with linen or sawdust, treating the body with a solution until the tissues dried out, and wrapping it in many layers of bandages.

◉ The New Kingdom

The New Kingdom (1550–1050 B.C.) began when Ahmoe I founded the eighteenth dynasty and expelled the Hyksos. Egypt developed a permanent army that borrowed horse-drawn chariots and other military techniques of the Hyksos. With improved weaponry, military forces—led by Thutmose I and Queen Hatshepsut—entered southwestern Asia.

Queen Hatshepsut also encouraged trade with other regions of Africa and oversaw the construction of magnificent temples and palaces.

When the queen's successor, Thutmose III, gained control of Egypt around 1480 B.C., his efforts were concentrated on military conquest. Within twenty years, he had conquered Palestine and Syria, pushing Egypt's northeastern frontier to the upper waters of the Euphrates River in Asia. One of the greatest triumphs of Egyptian might, the expanded empire survived for a century, making Thebes and Memphis political and cultural hubs of the ancient world.

During the mid-fourteenth century B.C., Amenhotep IV began to worship a sun god called Aten. He changed his name to Akhenaton and moved his court from Thebes to Tell al-Amarna. Akhenaton's concentration on religious affairs led to neglect of the empire. This enabled the Hittites of Asia Minor (modern Turkey) to take over Syria. Furthermore, priests of the old religion, who worshiped Amen as king of the gods, led revolts within Egypt. Akhenaton's successor, King Tutankhamen, made worship of Amen the official religion again.

The treasures found in the tomb of the pharaoh **Tutankhamen** are some of the most widely recognized artifacts in the world. Tutankhamen died at the age of eighteen. Many experts believe he may have been murdered by relatives who sought his throne.

The individual stone blocks used to build the **Great Pyramids at Giza** weigh between 2 and 15 tons (1.8 and 13.5 metric tons). More than 14 million sandstone blocks were used in the construction of these three pyramids.

THE PYRAMID BUILDERS

Before the Aswan High Dam was built in the late 1960s, the Nile flooded for three months each year, making it impossible for farmers to cultivate its banks. The pharaohs took advantage of this time by forcing peasant farmers to build monuments and other structures, including the Great Pyramids at Giza.

During the late New Kingdom, Egypt again prospered, recovering lost territories and renewing trade. King Seti I regained Palestine and Syria, and his son, Ramses II, fought the Hittites. But once again, Egypt was unable to retain its power as invaders came by sea from across the Mediterranean. Nubians from the south and Assyrians and Persians from the east dominated Egypt in succession.

◉ Greek and Roman Rule

In 332 B.C., the Greeks of the northern Mediterranean Sea conquered Egypt. Their ruler, Alexander the Great, founded the seaport of Alexandria in northern coastal Egypt. Under Greek rule, arts and trade flourished, and Alexandria became a hub of learning, religion, and commerce. Egypt's prosperity eventually attracted the Romans of central Italy, who conquered the country in 30 B.C., making it a Roman province.

Roman control continued in Egypt for several centuries. Christianity began to spread throughout Egypt in the first and the second centuries A.D. Egypt became an important center for Christianity and developed its own sect, called the Coptic Church, in the fifth century A.D.

Early Arab Rulers

Islam appeared as the world's third major monotheistic (single-god) religion—after Judaism and Christianity—during the early seventh century. Followers of the new religion were called Muslims. Based on the teachings of the prophet Muhammad, Islam spread quickly from the Arabian Peninsula into Syria and Palestine and then into Egypt. Egypt was very important to the Arabs because it was the major grain-producing region of their main adversary—the Byzantine, or Eastern Roman, Empire. In addition, Alexandria was a valuable base for the Byzantine navy.

In 639 the Arab commander Amr ibn al-As invaded Egypt from Syria. In 641 he captured Alexandria, Egypt's capital at the time. He then established a new capital at al-Fustat (later Old Cairo). Many of the Coptic Christians converted to Islam and began to intermarry with Arabs during the early Arab period in Egypt.

The conquest of Egypt launched Arab expansion into North Africa and into Spain. Gradually, a Muslim administration that used Arabic as its native language replaced the traditions that had prevailed since the Roman period.

The Arabs administered Egypt first from Damascus, Syria, during the Umayyad caliphate (a Muslim dynasty that lasted from 661 to 750) and thereafter from Baghdad, Iraq, the capital of the Abbasid rulers. In 868 the Abbasid caliph, or Islamic leader, appointed Ahmad ibn Tulun as the governor of Egypt. Ibn Tulun ruled wisely and effectively. He also established his own ruling family—taking advantage of a weakening Abbasid government—and controlled an independent empire that included Egypt, Palestine, and Syria. Tulunid rule ended in 905, when the Abbasids regained their authority.

Muslim conquerers usually gave their defeated foes three choices: convert to Islam; retain their own religion and pay a poll tax; or, face war and destruction. In time, most Egyptians accepted Islam, while a small but strong community of Coptic Christians retained its beliefs. This community still exists in Egypt.

During the tenth century, rivals to the Abbasids arose west of Egypt, in Tunisia. Called the Fatimids, they pursued an aggressive policy toward other Arab lands. In 969 the Fatimid leader Jawhar al-Siqilli captured Egypt from Abbasid control. Jawhar immediately laid out a new capital next to the older one at al-Fustat. He named the new city al-Qahirah, or Cairo ("the victorious"). It became the Fatimid capital in 973 as well as a major cultural and religious center for the Arab world.

The world's leading center of Islamic study, **al-Azhar University in Cairo** was founded by the Fatimids during the tenth century.

The Fatimid period in Egypt was one of extensive construction of mosques (Islamic houses of prayer), palaces, canals, and other public works projects. The Fatimids founded one of the first universities in the world, al-Azhar, which helped to make Cairo a major center of Islamic learning. Although the Fatimids were of the Shiite Muslim sect, they generally allowed Egyptians, who were predominantly Sunni Muslims, to continue Sunni beliefs. Later Fatimid rulers, however, faced serious problems. They were unable to control soldiers within the Fatimid army, and famine in 1065 further weakened their rule.

Crusaders from western Europe set out to establish Christianity in southwestern Asia during the twelfth century. To stem the flow of Christian armed forces, the Fatimid caliph in Egypt appealed to the sultan (ruler) of Syria in 1168 for assistance. The sultan sent an army to defend Egypt. Saladin, a general in the sultan's army, became vizier (a high official) of Egypt. In 1171 he overthrew the Fatimids and established the Ayyubid dynasty, restoring Sunni rule to Egypt. Saladin went on to reconquer Palestine, taking it back from the Crusaders. The Ayyubids remained in control of Egypt until 1250, when they were replaced by the Mamluks.

Mamluk and Ottoman Control

The Mamluks were people of Turkish, Mongolian, and Circassian origins who had been brought to Egypt as slaves by the Ayyubids. The sultan of Egypt had given the Mamluks special military training. They became his bodyguards and rose to high positions in the army and the government. This power enabled them to take over the sultan's domain. The Mamluks formed a military hierachy that ruled Egypt from 1250 until 1517.

Under Mamluk control, Egypt gained wealth and territory, expanding its boundaries northward to include Syria, mainland Turkey, and the island of Cyprus in the Mediterranean Sea. The Mamluks also made substantial contributions to Egyptian artistic culture, especially in the forms of bronze and brass work, enameled glass, pottery, and intricately decorated manuscripts.

In 1517 the Ottoman Turks conquered Egypt and initiated a period of influence that lasted through the middle of the seventeenth century. Although officially claimed as part of the Ottoman Empire until World War I (1914–1918), Egypt retained its own unique identity. Eventually, the country governed itself, independent of the far-off Turkish empire.

The Ottomans placed the country under the control of Turkish officials, called pashas, but the pashas participated little in the Egyptian government. The Ottomans also retained the Mamluks within the local administration. The Mamluks became beys, or regional governors, and held the real power in Egypt.

From the sixteenth to the mid-eighteenth centuries, Egypt prospered because it served as a stopping point along several trade routes between Europe and Asia. From 1770 to 1800, however, Egypt suffered from plagues and famine, and many Egyptians died.

Napoleon

In 1798 French troops led by Napoleon Bonaparte invaded Egypt. His goal was to achieve a strategic edge in the French war against Britain by gaining control of the shortest overland route to the British colony of India. Napoleon captured Alexandria and defeated the Mamluks at the Battle of the Pyramids. Three years later, however, the French were driven out of Egypt by a combined force of British and Ottoman soldiers. Although the French occupation was too short to have a lasting effect on Egypt, it renewed European interest in the area and left the country in a state of turmoil.

▶ Muhammad Ali Pasha and European Intervention

By 1805 a powerful figure had emerged in Egypt. Muhammad Ali Pasha—a young Albanian officer who had been sent by the Turkish sultan in 1801 to help oust the French—was appointed governor of Egypt. During the next forty years, Muhammad Ali instituted broad reforms to modernize Egypt. He changed the educational system by hiring foreign teachers to train people for modern administrative and military posts. He also established a health and sanitation board to control diseases. He developed manufacturing industries, encouraged the production of cotton, created a modern army, and began to change the way land was distributed.

To gain control of the trade routes into Egypt, Muhammad Ali embarked upon a program of expansion, adding Sudan and parts of Saudi Arabia to his realm around 1820. In 1831 he invaded Syria, defeating the Ottoman armies there, and then threatened to march on to Istanbul, the capital of the Ottoman Empire. Russia, Britain, and Austria intervened to protect the Turkish sultan, but they left Muhammad Ali in control of Syria and the island of Crete. When he attacked and defeated the sultan's armies again in 1839, the British organized an alliance to force him out of Syria. Muhammad Ali withdrew from Syria after the British offered him and his descendants permanent control over Egypt and Sudan.

Often referred to as the father of modern Egypt, **Muhammad Ali Pasha** instituted reforms in the Egyptian military, as well as in the economic, educational, and health care systems.

After the death of Muhammad Ali in 1849, Egypt increasingly came under European influence, as careless rulers nearly drove the country into bankruptcy. In 1859 the French Suez Canal Company under Ferdinand-Marie de Lesseps began building the Suez Canal to shorten the water route between Europe and India. The immense task, which took a decade to complete, further drained Egypt's financial resources. Egypt agreed to let the Suez Canal Company operate the canal for ninety-nine years. Stock in the canal was owned chiefly by Egypt and France.

In 1875, however, Egypt was forced to sell its share of the company to the British government to repay foreign loans. The sale did not prove sufficient to satisfy Egypt's creditors. In 1876 a British-French commission took charge of Egypt's finances, and in 1879 the Ottoman sultan replaced the country's ruler, Ismail Pasha, with his son, Tawfiq Pasha. In 1882, when the Egyptian army rebelled against foreign control, the British occupied Egypt.

Although Egypt technically was still part of the Ottoman Empire when World War I began, Great Britain made the country a protectorate (dependent political unit) in 1914 after the Ottomans sided with the Germans in the war. Britain's occupation intensified, focusing on the Suez Canal as the keystone to strategic planning in the region.

The war years were difficult for many Egyptians. Inflation increased, as did resentment toward British control. Egyptian activists formed a nationalist movement called the Wafd ("delegation") in 1918. When the British exiled Sa'd Zaghlul, the Wafd leader, Egyptian citizens revolted.

◉ Independence

Great Britain declared Egypt's independence in 1922. Fuad I, the sultan of Egypt, became the new nation's king and worked alongside an elected parliament. Although the country was independent in name, its foreign policy was still tightly tied to that of Great Britain, and British troops remained in the country. These arrangements robbed Egypt of true independence. Although an Anglo-Egyptian treaty was signed in 1936, British troops remained in the Suez Canal Zone.

Italian and German troops tried to capture the Suez Canal during World War II (1939–1945), but British forces drove them out. With British backing, the Wafd briefly controlled Egypt from 1942 to 1944. But its cooperation with the British, as well as revelations of corruption, diminished the Wafd's popular support. Meanwhile, fundamentalist (conservative) religious organizations, such as the Muslim Brotherhood and Young Egypt, gained popularity, as Egyptians became disillusioned with the Wafd and other internal issues.

The Suez Canal extends from Port Said to Port Taufiq and connects the Mediterranean Sea with the Gulf of Suez and with the Red Sea. The canal is more than 100 miles (160 km) long.

In 1945 Egypt and six other nations founded the Arab League, which made its headquarters in Cairo. The League looked forward to an era when Arabs could establish unity and control their own destiny. Conflict within the Middle East, however, was renewed in November 1947. At that time, the United Nations (UN) recommended that Palestine be partitioned (divided) into two states—a Jewish state and a Palestinian Arab state.

The Zionist movement—which sought to create a Jewish homeland in Palestine—had begun in the late 1800s. Although Arabs had been concerned about Jewish immigration into the region, Great Britain assured them that the new presence did not pose a threat to their territories.

However, when the partition plan was announced, the Arab world refused to accept it. Egypt, Syria, Lebanon, and Transjordan (later Jordan) declared war on the new Jewish State of Israel on May 14, 1948. Israel defeated the Arab alliance, extending its borders into part of the proposed Palestinian state. Transjordan annexed the rest of the territory that had been set aside for the Palestinian Arabs. Egypt captured the Gaza Strip along the Mediterranean Sea.

◉ The 1952 Revolution

The persistent British presence, the military and political consequences of Israel's creation, and the corruption associated with the regime of King Farouk—who had succeeded Fuad I—eventually caused disturbances within Egypt. Student riots increased, and a military coup took place on July 23, 1952. Major General Muhammad Naguib and Colonel Gamal Abdel Nasser led the coup. In 1953 Egypt was declared a republic, and the following year Nasser assumed the post of prime minister. (He would be elected president in 1956.) The new regime immediately embarked on an era of change, starting with redistribution of land, removal of foreign troops, and economic reform.

Nasser's socialist approach to government was based on a desire to improve the lives of Egypt's citizens. But he also undermined personal freedom and discouraged dissent by outlawing all political parties and imprisoning critics of his government.

In 1954 the British gave in to Nasser's demands and agreed to remove all of their troops by 1956. An agreement with the Soviet Union in 1955 assured Egypt of large imports of jet warplanes, rifles, and tanks for defense of the nation. Although this tie with the Communist bloc worried countries in Europe and North America, Nasser's policies were more concerned with the Arab world, with Islam, and with African affairs.

The Suez War

In mid-1956, the United States and Britain withdrew offers made in December 1955 to help build a huge new dam across the Nile River near Aswan. Both countries stated that Egypt was not strong enough economically to make the costly project a profitable venture. In response, Nasser nationalized (changed to state ownership) the Suez Canal, which had been owned by Britain and France. In so doing, Egypt intended to use tolls collected from the waterway to finance construction of the Aswan High Dam. The move angered Britain and France.

During this period, relations with Israel worsened. Egypt continued to block Israeli ships from both the Suez Canal and the Gulf of Aqaba, a move that cut off Israel's sea communications to the west. In addition, Israel accused Egypt of supplying financial aid and arms to Palestinian commandos, who were attacking Israeli settlements. Thus, Israel became a natural ally for Britain and France. The three countries attacked Egypt in 1956. When the Suez War—known in Egypt as the Tripartite Aggression—broke out, Israel quickly occupied

Fighting during the Suez War left areas of Port Said in ruins.

most of the Sinai Peninsula. After British and French troops invaded the canal zone, the UN stepped in to end the fighting. It stationed an emergency force on the Egyptian side of the Sinai border and at Sharm al-Sheikh, at the tip of the peninsula.

Although Egypt had been defeated in the war, Nasser's stand against the British, French, and Israelis made him a hero in Egypt and the Arab world. Soon thereafter, Nasser secured financing from the Soviet Union for the Aswan High Dam. The deal began a period of close ties between the Egyptians and the Soviets.

NASSER AND THE NONALIGNED MOVEMENT

In the mid-1950s, the Cold War was brewing between the Communist Soviet Union and democracies such as the United States and Great Britain. The rival nations called upon other nations of the world to take sides in the conflict. At that time, Egyptian president Gamal Abdel Nasser became a leader in the Nonaligned Movement, a group of nations that rejected alliances with either side. Other nations in this movement—which sought to avoid being embroiled in conflicts between the two world powers—included Yugoslavia, China, India, Cuba, Iraq, and Indonesia. By siding with neither group, Nasser hoped to receive aid and purchase weapons from both. But the democracies demanded an alliance and refused to aid or supply Egypt with weapons. This caused Nasser to turn to the Soviet Union for support.

⊙ Unity and Conflict

In 1958 Nasser merged Egypt with Syria to form the United Arab Republic. Although the two countries are separated geographically, Nasser believed that a union between Syria and Egypt would be a step toward a greater level of Arab unity.

Dissatisfaction set in among Syrians, however, much of it based on Nasser's socialist policies. In 1961 a group of Syrian officers rebelled and declared Syria an independent state. This was a great blow to Nasser, who tried to quell the uprising with his troops, but eventually he accepted the loss of Syria. Egypt, nevertheless, retained the name of the United Arab Republic until 1971, when the name of Egypt was restored.

During the spring of 1967, at Nasser's request, the UN withdrew its troops along the Sinai-Negev border. Nasser then advanced his army and again, as in 1956, ordered the Gulf of Aqaba closed to Israeli shipping. Egypt also signed a military alliance with Syria and Jordan.

Faced with threats of war, Israel

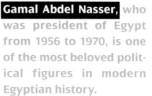

Gamal Abdel Nasser, who was president of Egypt from 1956 to 1970, is one of the most beloved political figures in modern Egyptian history.

attacked all three Arab states at once on June 5, 1967, taking over the Sinai Peninsula from Egypt—as well as other territories held by Jordan and Syria—in six days. Nasser offered to resign his position after the defeat in the Six-Day War, but the Egyptian people took to the streets by the thousands to show support for their president. Nasser withdrew his resignation.

Although the war had ended, fighting continued along the Suez Canal, which had been closed during the conflict. In August 1970, Egypt and Israel agreed to a temporary cease-fire, in the hope of beginning peace talks in the near future. Nasser's sudden death from a heart attack in September 1970, however, disrupted the plans.

Anwar el-Sadat and Peace with Israel

Vice President Anwar el-Sadat succeeded Nasser as president. Sadat released political dissenters who had been imprisoned by Nasser and set out to liberalize Egypt's economy and government. He decreased censorship of the press, which Nasser had strictly controlled, and ordered all Soviet military advisers out of Egypt during the summer of 1972.

Anwar el-Sadat

In October 1973, Egypt and Syria attacked Israel to gain back territories lost in 1967. The two countries took Israel by surprise, attacking on Yom Kippur, the holiest day of the Jewish year. The war ended after eighteen days of fighting, when the UN imposed a cease-fire. Although the Egyptian forces performed well at the outset, overrunning part of the Sinai Peninsula, the Israelis had regained the initiative when the cease-fire was called. Nevertheless, Egypt's effective challenge to the 1967 boundaries restored the nation's image of strength, and Sadat felt able to negotiate with Israel.

By the summer of 1974, Egypt and Israel had agreed to exchange prisoners and to set up buffer zones using UN forces. These agreements permitted the Egyptians to begin work on reopening the Suez Canal, which occurred in 1975. More significantly, however, the peace negotiations resulted in the return to Egypt of part of the Sinai Peninsula and provided the basis for an Egyptian-Israeli peace treaty.

In 1977 Sadat announced his historic decision to go to Jerusalem to address the Israeli Knesset (parliament) about a peace settlement. Although Sadat's visit opened the door to the peacemaking process, it caused many frustrations—including the isolation imposed on Egypt by other Arab states that resented Egypt's negotiations with Israel.

In 1978 U.S. president Jimmy Carter invited Israeli prime minister Menachem Begin and President Sadat to Camp David, Maryland. There they constructed a framework for peace between the two countries. A treaty—which Egypt and Israel signed on March 26, 1979,

The Camp David Accords were signed by Egyptian president Anwar el-Sadat *(seated left)*, U.S. president Jimmy Carter *(seated center)*, and Israeli prime minister Menachem Begin *(seated right)* in Washington, D.C., on March 26, 1979.

in Washington, D.C.—ended their state of war. As a result of the treaty, diplomatic relations between the two nations were established, and Israel returned all of the Sinai Peninsula to Egypt. The rest of the Arab world branded Sadat a traitor to the Arab cause, and Egypt was expelled from the Arab League.

After 1979 Sadat met with increasing opposition within Egypt. The country's dismal economy failed to improve. While Sadat's "open-door" policy of encouraging foreign investment made some Egyptians wealthy, most Egyptians saw no improvement in their lives. In response to criticisms of his regime, Sadat restricted the Egyptian press and imprisoned those who spoke against his policies. Many of his opponents were Islamic fundamentalists. On October 6, 1981, members of an Islamic fundamentalist group assassinated Sadat while he was reviewing Egyptian troops.

Hosni Mubarak

Anwar el-Sadat was succeeded as president by Vice President Muhammad Hosni Mubarak. Mubarak promised to support the peace treaty with Israel and to concentrate more on problems within Egypt. He also worked on strengthening ties with other Arab states. At the Arab summit meeting in November 1987, most Arab leaders agreed to end Egypt's isolation, and within two years Egypt was readmitted to the Arab League.

The early 1990s brought additional international challenges to the Mubarak administration. In August 1990, Iraq invaded Kuwait, an oil-rich nation along the Persian Gulf in the Middle East. The Iraqi army took over the Kuwaiti capital and stationed troops throughout the country. Arab League members were at odds about the appropriate course of action to take. The UN voted to impose economic penalties, called sanctions, on Iraq and left open the possibility of sending an international military force into Kuwait.

SADAT'S LEGACY

Decades after his assassination, Anwar el-Sadat remains a controversial figure in Egypt. A 2001 documentary film about his life, *Days of Sadat*, has reignited debate among Egyptians over Sadat and his rule. While some continue to condemn his 1979 peace agreement with Israel, claiming the action was a betrayal of a united Arab cause, others see the agreement as a visionary first step toward peace in the Middle East. Sadat's critics also continue to take issue with his domestic policies, which they feel led to corruption and a growing disparity between rich and poor. Sadat's defenders argue that Egypt had no choice but to abandon Nasser's socialist policies, which were not achieving the desired goals.

 35

Hosni Mubarak succeeded Anwar el-Sadat as Egypt's president. He had previously served as vice president, deputy minister of war, and chief of staff of the Egyptian Air Force.

Egypt, as well as most other Arab nations, supported the UN sanctions as a means of resolving the Persian Gulf crisis without bloodshed. Eventually, however, Saudi Arabia feared for its own safety. It asked for protection from the United States, which formed a military coalition with several European and Arab nations to reclaim Kuwait. President Mubarak supported the coalition, sending 30,000 Egyptian troops to Saudi Arabia.

Egypt's participation in the military coalition had many economic benefits. European, U.S., and Arab leaders erased one-third of Egypt's foreign debt. Grants poured in from rich oil-producing Arab states, such as Saudi Arabia, and international banks arranged new loans. In addition, Egypt's own oil industry experienced a boom as warfare cut off oil sources elsewhere in the Persian Gulf.

By the time the Gulf crisis had ended in mid-1991, Egypt was in a stronger economic position. To foster economic progress, Mubarak tried to balance the needs of Egypt's large number of low-income citizens with measures to end subsidies (government payments) for basic consumer goods.

Despite some economic success in the early 1990s, the Egyptian economy has not kept up with its rapidly growing population. Extreme social ills in Egypt have led to the rise of Islamic fundamentalist groups, whose goal is to create a state based on Islamic law. The largest of these groups is the Muslim Brotherhood, which, although banned since 1954, has hundreds of thousands of members. The brotherhood advocates the overthrow of the Egyptian government by political means.

However, another organization known as the Islamic Group has used terrorism to try to achieve an Islamic state. In the past, the Islamic Group has targeted President Mubarak and other Egyptian political figures for assassination and has killed or wounded hundreds of people, primarily civilians and tourists, in terrorist attacks. In September and November of 1997, the Islamic Group staged two attacks on tourists in Cairo and Luxor, killing seventy-nine people. The attacks devastated the Egyptian tourism industry, causing further damage to the economy. The Egyptian government responded by imposing strong security measures, including detaining suspects without trial, and alleged use of torture. These actions have drawn protest from human rights groups. Terrorist attacks have diminished considerably in recent years as antigovernment groups have sought to influence policy through political means.

◉ Moving into the Future

President Mubarak was elected to a fourth term in 1999. While the country's population growth seems to be slowing, Egypt's economy is still struggling to keep pace. Included in Mubarak's agenda is an ambitious plan to reclaim millions of acres of desert for farming, through the building of canals and the tapping of an aquifer deep beneath the Western Desert. Several of these projects were launched in 1997 and are scheduled for completion in the first decade of the twenty-first century.

Irrigation devices, like this **aquifer drainage channel,** are an important part of President Hosni Mubarak's ambitious agricultural reform agenda.

The Mubarak government immediately condemned the September 11, 2001, terrorist attacks on the United States, in which Islamic radicals crashed fuel-laden airliners into the World Trade Center in New York City and the Pentagon in Arlington, Virginia, killing thousands. (On that day, a fourth airliner crashed in rural Pennsylvania, after passengers on board the plane presumably wrested control of it from terrorists determined to crash it into another U.S. landmark.) Cairo's al-Azhar University, the world's leading authority on Sunni Islamic law, also condemned the terrorist acts.

International intelligence sources allege that the organizers and perpetrators of the attacks were members of a worldwide terrorist network called al-Qaeda, whose leader—Saudi-born millionaire Osama bin Laden—was based in Afghanistan. Weeks after the attacks, the United States launched a military campaign in Afghanistan against al-Qaeda and the Taliban, the Afghan regime that was harboring bin Laden and al-Qaeda. A significant number of Egyptians are believed to be members of al-Qaeda, whose aim is to wage jihad, or holy war, against the United States. Two Egyptian exiles, Muhammad Atef and Ayman al-Zawahri, were known to be high-ranking figures in the organization. Atef was reported killed during a U.S. airstrike in Afghanistan in November 2001. Another Egyptian, Muhammad Atta, is alleged to have been the ringleader of the groups that hijacked the aircraft and may have been piloting one of the planes that destroyed the World Trade Center.

The Egyptian government has assisted the United States in its investigation of the attacks, providing intelligence about al-Qaeda and other terrorist organizations. In return, the Mubarak regime has

Two Egyptians, **Ayman al-Zawahri *(left)* and Muhammad Atef *(right)*,** have served as top deputies in Osama bin Laden's *(center)* al-Qaeda terrorist network. Atef was reportedly killed by U.S. forces in Afghanistan in 2001.

requested that the United States take a leadership role in the dispute between Israel and the Palestinians. This dispute is the major source of conflict in the Middle East and a key component of anti-American sentiment among many communities in the region. Many Arabs blame the Israeli-Palestinian conflict on the United States, which supports Israel both economically and militarily. The United States has promised Egypt economic assistance for its help in the war on terrorism.

◉ Government

Egypt became a republic after the 1952 Revolution. The constitution, last revised in 1971, allows for only one person to run for president. At least two-thirds of Egypt's legislature and a majority of the voters must approve the president, who may serve an unlimited number of six-year terms. All Egyptians over the age of eighteen are obligated to vote.

The president is commander in chief of the army and may appoint one or more vice presidents and a cabinet. The chief executive may also dismiss these aides and the legislature at any time. The cabinet includes the prime minister and several vice premiers and ministers. This council helps the president to plan and direct national policy.

> To learn more about the Egyptian presidency, visit vgsbooks.com for a link where you can find a biography of Egypt's current president, a history of the office, news reports, and up-to-date policies, as well as a tour of the presidential palaces.

The Egyptian legislature, which is called the People's Assembly, has 454 members, 444 of whom are elected and 10 of whom are appointed by the president. The constitution reserves 50 percent of the seats for workers and farm laborers. Members of the assembly hold office for five-year terms and are empowered to approve the budget, make investigations, impose taxes, and endorse government programs.

Egypt's independent judicial system is based on elements of Islamic, British, and French laws. In 1956 Egypt became the first Arab country to abolish Islamic and other religious courts. A supreme court is the most powerful of Egypt's four categories of courts. Below the supreme court are the court of cassation (the highest court of appeal), lower courts of appeal, and tribunals.

Each of Egypt's twenty-six governorates (provinces) is headed by a governor who is appointed by the president. Councils, most of whose members are elected, assist the governors. Cities and villages also have elected councils, which are headed by mayors.

THE PEOPLE

With a population of 68.3 million, Egypt is the most populous country in the Arab world and the second most populous—after Nigeria—on the African continent. Most of the population is concentrated in villages and cities along the Nile. Egypt's large population puts tremendous pressure on natural resources and food supplies. A large percentage of Egyptians have low incomes. According to a 1999 estimate, as many as 35 percent of Egyptians are living below the poverty line.

Ethnic Groups

The vast majority of Egyptians—99 percent—are of Hamitic ancestry. Hamites are descendants of the ancient Egyptians, but Egypt's long history of occupation by foreign peoples has resulted in a long and complicated intermingling of ethnic groups. Thus, the term Egyptian is a difficult one to define. Most Egyptians refer to themselves as Arabs.

Egyptian minorities include the Nubians of southern Egypt and the Bedouin people, many of whom live in the Western Desert and on the Sinai Peninsula. A large portion of the Nubian population lost their traditional way of life when the Aswan High Dam was built. The dam's reservoir, Lake Nasser, flooded the region that had been Nubian farmland for thousands of years. The Egyptian government has sponsored programs to resettle the Nubians in different parts of the country. Many have also moved to Egypt's urban areas in search of employment.

The Bedouin have traditionally traveled throughout the desert in search of fresh pasture for their sheep and goats. They use camels as their main form of transportation. Camels also provide Bedouin with milk, and camel hair is used to make rugs, clothing, and tents. Recent generations of Bedouin have adopted a farming lifestyle. The Egyptian government has encouraged this trend by providing schools and medical facilities for the Bedouin.

Way of Life

Rural Egyptians make up 56 percent of the total population and are primarily low-income farm laborers, called *fellahin*. Many fellahin live in homes built with mud bricks that have been dried in the sun, although houses made of cement blocks are becoming more common. Fellahin generally live in crowded villages along the Nile River and farm small patches of land. Most families own a small number of farm animals, such as goats, chickens, and sheep. The Egyptian

Rural children

government has sent professionals from Cairo and other large cities to rural villages to teach the local people modern methods of agriculture.

Most people who live in Egyptian cities are unskilled laborers who do not earn much money. Many work two or three jobs in order to make ends meet. Most make their homes in the older sections of cities in crowded, tightly packed buildings. Often these urban workers own a few domestic animals such as chickens, sheep, and goats, which they depend on for milk and eggs. Some of these workers manage to make enough money to enter Egypt's growing middle class, which is composed mostly of merchants, financiers, and technicians. Small groups of

Many of Egypt's rural families live in mud brick houses, like these in Luxor.

wealthy landowners and military officers live in urban areas as well. Their houses and lifestyles are similar to those of wealthy people in other parts of Africa or in Europe. Wealthier Egyptians are the major consumers of European and American cars, films, music, and fashion.

Health

Health services vary greatly among Egyptians, depending on a family's income and education. Basic health care needs, such as doctor visits and hospital stays, are paid for by the government. But most public health clinics and hospitals lack basic equipment, and many other health-related expenses—such as medicine and bandages—are not paid for by the government. Wealthier Egyptians often visit private health facilities.

Many poor Egyptians suffer from malnutrition due to an inadequate diet, which often consists of bread made from corn, sorghum (a cereal grain), or wheat; dates; and a small amount of *kishk* (a paste made from sour milk and flour). An estimated 20 percent of Egyptian children suffer from stuntedness (lack of proper growth), a sign of malnutrition.

Health statistics suggest that conditions in Egypt are average for northern Africa. The infant mortality rate of 52 deaths for every 1,000 live births and the life expectancy of 65 years of age are similar to other nations of the region. The rapid growth in population is also typical, although Egypt's 1.9 percent annual rate of population increase is slightly lower than that of other North African countries. This lower birthrate is the result of the government's family planning initiatives, which have encouraged the use of contraceptives and have made them readily available. An estimated 47 percent of Egyptian couples are practicing contraception, and the government's goal is to increase this number to 70 percent by 2010.

At the beginning of the twenty-first century, Egypt faces a major epidemic of the hepatitis C virus. Public health officials estimate that as many as 15 to 20 percent of Egypt's population has been exposed to the

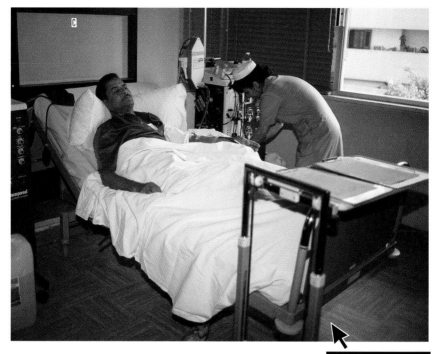

Although health care is funded by the government, many **Egyptian hospitals** struggle to meet the demands of a growing population.

virus, which can cause serious, even fatal, liver disease. Ironically, the hepatitis C epidemic is believed to have been caused by public health officials themselves. From 1961 to 1986, millions of Egyptians were given injections of tartar emetic—a remedy for a disease called bilharzia that was plaguing rural areas of the country at the time. Officials frequently reused needles without sterilizing them first—leading to the spread of hepatitis C, a virus for which there is no known cure.

Egypt has had fewer documented cases of HIV/AIDS than many African countries. A 2000 study by the UN and the World Health Organization listed 8,100 cases of HIV/AIDS in Egypt. Egypt's conservative Islamic culture— which strongly discourages both sexual promiscuity and drug use— is a key factor in the low rate of infection.

Bilharzia, also called schistosomiasis, is a disease that afflicts more than 200 million people worldwide. It is prevalent in the Nile Valley and 5 percent of Egyptians suffer from it. Bilharzia is spread when infected humans urinate or defecate in fresh water. The contaminated water then infects others. The disease causes abdominal pain, coughing, fever, nausea, and rashes. Severe cases can damage the liver, spleen, and intestines.

Education

Prior to the 1800s, basic education in Egypt was administered by churches and mosques. The curriculum usually consisted of reading, writing, arithmetic, and memorization of passages of the Quran (the holy book of Islam) or Bible. In the early 1800s, Muhammad Ali Pasha established a modern secular education system to train Egyptian men for civil service work. This system was expanded in the second half of the century with the creation of public schools at the primary, secondary, and higher education levels. Egypt's first school for girls was established in 1873. For the most part during this period, education was available only to the wealthy.

Following the 1952 Revolution, the Egyptian government pledged to provide free education to all Egyptians. The Egyptian educational system grew tremendously from the 1950s through the mid-1970s. Thousands of new schools were built during this period. In recent decades, budget concerns have hampered the progress of the Egyptian educational system.

The Egyptian Ministry of Education trains teachers, builds schools, and offers free education from the primary through the university level. Not enough facilities exist for all children to attend classes, however.

This group of schoolgirls lives in Kom Ombo, about 31 miles (50 km) north of Aswan.

Often, schools will teach two or three different groups of students in morning, afternoon, and evening shifts. Teacher salaries are so low that instructors are forced to supplement their incomes with private tutoring.

Because the state-funded educational system isn't adequately preparing students, private lessons sometimes become mandatory for advancement to the next academic level. This situation leaves many low-income parents with the difficult choice of deciding which of their children can afford tutoring and which cannot. In most such cases, boys receive the additional lessons, while girls do not receive a full education. As a result, studies show a marked disparity in literacy rates between Egyptian men and women. While 64 percent of Egyptian men can read, only 39 percent of Egyptian women are literate. Furthermore, some children are unable to attend classes because their parents need them to work in the fields. About 80 percent of all children are enrolled in primary school, but only 68 percent continue on to high school.

Most of the postsecondary institutions in Egypt are located in or near Cairo. Egypt has fifteen free universities, which are controlled by the Ministry of Higher Education. There is one private university, the American University of Cairo, which was founded by Americans in 1919 and teaches undergraduate, graduate, and professional courses in

English. Al-Azhar University is the oldest Islamic educational institution in the world. More than 90,000 students from around the world study at al-Azhar, which is considered the leading authority of Sunni Muslim Sharia (Islamic law). The school also offers courses in Arabic studies, agriculture, medicine, and engineering.

> If you'd like to learn more about al-Azhar University, the world's leading Islamic learning institution, go to vgsbooks.com to find a link.

Language

About 98 percent of Egyptians speak Arabic, Egypt's official language. French and English are also spoken in Egypt, particularly among the educated classes. Arabic is a Semitic language that originated on the Arabian Peninsula and was brought to Egypt during the Arab conquest. The Arabic alphabet has 28 characters and is read from right to left and from the top to the bottom of a page. Nearly 200 million people speak Arabic worldwide.

Spoken Arabic is quite different than written Arabic. Written, or classical, Arabic is the language of the Quran. It is used in newspapers, books, and other writing and is virtually the same throughout the Arab region. Spoken, or colloquial, Arabic has nine major dialects, two of which—Egyptian and South Egyptian—are spoken in Egypt. These dialects differ in their use of vocabulary, pronunciation, grammar, and sentence structure.

This imposing gate leads to the oldest Muslim university in the world, **Al-Azhar University.**

CULTURAL LIFE

Egyptian culture is as diverse as it is unique. Daily life on the streets of Cairo is bustling and crowded, a stark contrast to the quiet life on the farms of the Nile Valley or the difficult conditions of desert-inhabiting nomads. Religion is a vital part of the lives of most Egyptians, although many citizens struggle to find a balance between secular and religious values.

◎ Religion

Islam, the faith of nearly 94 percent of the Egyptian population, is the official religion of the country. Most Egyptian Muslims belong to the Sunni sect. Since its founding in the tenth century, Cairo has been one of the great centers for religious study in the Muslim world. The city has more than one thousand mosques and many schools of Islamic learning, including al-Azhar University, the world's leading authority on Islamic law.

Muezzins, or criers, call Muslims to prayer five times a day, and

Egyptians are commonly seen praying in mosques, in markets, and in shopping centers. During the holy month of Ramadan and during other holy days, the recitation of the Quran can be heard in city streets over public address systems. The Quran is read on television, and the call to prayer is broadcast over loudspeakers, on the radio, and on television.

Islam in its original form combined government and religion. When the modern state system came into existence after World War I, government in Egypt became much more secularized. Many contemporary Muslims, however, object to the separation of religion and government. These people, generally called fundamentalists, want the Sharia, or Islamic law courts, installed as the tribunals of Egypt.

One reason for the growth of fundamentalism is the government's failure to improve the Egyptian standard of living. Fundamentalists want to develop cooperative organizations to establish more economic equality in Egyptian society. They also believe women should cover themselves as the Quran commands, and they stress the ideals of the past—when Arabs were unified and led the world in scientific achievement. Clashes between fundamentalists and the government have frequently occurred.

Small numbers of various Christian sects also exist in Egypt. Coptic Christians represent the country's largest minority religion. Under Byzantine rule, Egyptians developed their own branch of Christianity and broke away from the Roman Catholic Church during the sixth century. Most other Christians believe that Jesus was one person with two natures—one godly, one human. The Copts believe that Jesus had only a godly nature. Thus, the Copts became known as Monophysites, which literally means "one nature."

Egyptian Copts sit under a fresco depicting Joseph, Mary, and baby Jesus.

The Coptic **Church of Saints Peter and Paul,** built in 1911, is located in the northern part of Cairo.

Comprising about 6 percent of Egypt's population, the Copts are concentrated in the Coptic section of Cairo, in Luxor, and in Asyut. Tensions occurred between Copts and Muslim fundamentalists in the early 1980s and again in the mid-1990s, but President Mubarak has since adopted a policy of toleration toward the Copts.

Architecture

The Pyramids of Giza and the Temple of Luxor are considered to be among the greatest feats of ancient architecture anywhere. Visitors are still amazed by the sheer size of the Pyramids of Giza—the largest of the three, the Great Pyramid of Khufu, is built from an estimated 2.3 million stone blocks, each weighing an average of 2.5 tons (2.3 metric tons).

Cairo has the largest array of medieval Islamic architecture in the world. The city's oldest Islamic structure is the Mosque of Amr, which dates to A.D. 642. The most distinctive features of mosques are their minarets (tall, slender towers) and domes. Muezzins call Muslims to prayer from minarets. Cairo has been called the city of one thousand minarets because of its abundance of mosques. Domes are often decorated with elaborate zigzag, star, and floral patterns.

Aside from newer mosques, most contemporary Egyptian architecture lacks the distinction of earlier construction. Many buildings from

Many Muslim mosques, such as this one in Luxor, are adorned with tall towers called **minarets.** Muezzins, or criers, call Muslims to prayer five times each day from the balconies found at the top of minarets.

the 1800s and 1900s were designed and built with less care than in ancient and medieval times. The spectacular new Alexandria Library, completed in 2002, is already considered a wonder of modern architecture.

Literature, Television, and Film

Egypt has oral and written traditions that date back to the ancient pharaohs. The literary writings of ancient Egypt exhibit a wide diversity of forms and subjects. Some are poems, and others are letters. Still others are collections of moral instructions, which served as school texts that were copied by students to teach them to read and write. Some of the stories use elements of Egyptian mythology and probably originated as part of an oral storytelling tradition. As foreign conquerors took over the region, new styles and themes influenced writing. The literary classics read in Egypt in modern times include

Coptic and Arabic contributions as well as ancient works.

European culture has heavily influenced modern Egyptian literary trends. Contemporary Egyptian authors have adopted European prose forms, such as the short story, novel, and drama. The government has provided financial support to short-story writers, because it recognizes that literature not only spreads culture but also encourages Egyptians to participate in modern life.

Alongside these new forms, however, poetry remains popular, perhaps because it is easily remembered and transmitted by word of mouth. Furthermore, traditional poems were written to entertain ordinary people rather than to appeal to an elite class of educated thinkers.

One of Egypt's leading writers is Naguib Mahfouz. Best known for his Cairo Trilogy, a series of books that follows the lives of a Cairene family through the first half of the twentieth century, Mahfouz has written dozens of novels and short stories. In 1988 he became the first Arabic-language writer to win the Nobel Prize for Literature. Taha Hussein is another noted Egyptian writer. Author of a wide range of books, Hussein supervised the translation into Arabic of the complete works of Shakespeare. He died in 1973 at the age of eighty-four, the day after he received the UN prize for human rights.

Egyptians have access to a wide variety of **newspapers and magazines.**

Television and movies are an important part of Egyptian culture, particularly in urban areas. Televisions are found in 90 percent of Cairene households. Cairo is known as the Hollywood of the Arab world, producing films and television programs that are shown throughout the Middle East. The Egyptian government owns and controls the country's television industry. It imposes strict censorship of the airwaves and does not allow any morally or politically controversial programming. Programs include game shows, sitcoms, and serial dramas. Cairo's film studios produce about twenty movies a year, covering an array of topics and themes, from ancient Egyptian history to romantic comedies. Like television programming, Egyptian film is also strictly censored by the government. Yousef Chahine is the country's most distinguished film director. His works, which include *Al-Masir* and *Al-Widaa Bonaparte,* have received worldwide acclaim.

Marriage, Social Life, and Customs

As 94 percent of Egyptians are Muslim, many of the country's customs are dictated by the Quran. The Quran allows men to have as many as four wives, provided he is capable of supporting them. Most Egyptian men have just one. In the past, marriages were arranged by the bride and groom's families. This has changed in recent generations, however, particularly in Egypt's urban areas. Yet young men and women are seldom allowed to go out together without adult supervision.

Any marriage almost always requires the approval of both parties' parents. Often, the prospective groom will approach the bride's father, asking him for permission to marry his daughter. If the father of the bride approves, an engagement ceremony takes place, in which a section of the Quran is read. Before marriage the groom is usually

Elaborate weddings are an important part of modern Egyptian culture.

required to provide a dowry—a certain amount of money—which is a form of security for the bride, to discourage divorce. The Muslim wedding ceremony involves the signing of a contract between the groom and the bride's father. Afterward, a great celebration takes place.

Egyptian women enjoy more freedom than women in many Islamic countries. They are allowed to own land, drive vehicles, pursue higher education, and vote. They are not required to wear veils in public as are women in more conservative countries. Egyptian women are active in the fields of medicine, academics, art, journalism, and government.

Festivals and Food

Because Egypt is an Islamic country, holidays and festivals follow Islamic traditions. During the holy month of Ramadan, for example, Muslims fast from dawn to dusk each day. They mark the end of Ramadan with a three-day festival. Other festivals relate to historical events in Islam. The hegira, for example, celebrates the prophet Muhammad's escape from Mecca to Medina (both in Saudi Arabia) in the year 622 and marks the Islamic New Year.

Egyptians consider eating to be a social event, and meals take time and are prepared with care. A fancy meal may start with an assortment of smoked sardines, stuffed eggs, tiny meat-filled rolls, and beans

Egyptians enjoy food with plenty of strong **spices,** which are often sold in bulk at markets like this one in Cairo.

mixed with olive oil. Wealthier Egyptians eat a great deal of rice and mutton. Yellow saffron rice topped with boiled lamb is a popular dish. The diet of most Egyptians is based heavily on grains, which are supplemented with small amounts of dairy products and fruits, such as dates and figs.

Egyptians prepare highly seasoned foods using a variety of local spices. Menus often include grape leaves stuffed with rice. At celebrations, overflowing tables may feature a roasted loin of lamb, stuffed spiced chickens, shish kebabs, and continuous supplies of flat, round, freshly baked bread called *aysh.* Salads, fresh fruit, and sweets often complete the meal.

FUL MEDAMES

Ful medames, or fava bean breakfast spread, is usually served on pita bread. Fava beans are an important part of the Egyptian diet.

1 15-ounce can fava beans
1½ tablespoons olive oil
1 large onion, chopped
1 large tomato, diced
1 teaspoon ground cumin

¼ cup fresh parsley, chopped
¼ cup fresh lemon juice
salt and pepper to taste
ground red pepper to taste

Pour beans into a pot and bring to a boil. Mix the beans well and reduce heat. Add remaining ingredients, mixing well. Bring mixture to boil again. Reduce heat to medium. Cook for 5 minutes. Serve warm with warm pita bread.

Makes 6 servings.

◉ Sports and Recreation

Sports, especially soccer, are very popular in Egypt. Like many other soccer-mad nations, normal life in Egypt comes to a near standstill during important matches. Coaches and players can face immense pressure from fans, and while important wins bring huge celebrations in the streets, crucial losses have resulted in minor violence and property damage.

Egypt has long participated in the Olympic Games, with Egyptians winning medals in 1928 and 1936. The country sent athletes to compete in the 1996 Atlanta games and in the 2000 Sydney games for sports such as men's handball, Greco-Roman wrestling, boxing, rowing, swimming, and judo.

In addition to spectator sports, Egyptians enjoy a variety of different recreational games and activities, including basketball, volleyball, polo, squash, bicycling, and tennis. As popular as these activities are among many Egyptians, however, perhaps the most popular way to spend free time is in the company of family and friends. Men in Cairo and other Egyptian cities enjoy spending time in cafés, chatting about the latest news or sports event.

Egypt's **Mohamed Omara (center)** fights for the ball during the African Nations Cup soccer match in Mali. Soccer is the most popular sport in Egypt.

THE ECONOMY

Considered the breadbasket of both the Roman and Byzantine Empires, Egypt historically has lived on its agricultural harvests. Even in modern times, the foundation of Egypt's economy rests largely on its 7 million acres (2.8 million hectares) of Nile farmland. About half the population lives in rural areas and works in the farming sector. Before the 1952 Revolution, agriculture accounted for up to 80 percent of the nation's exports. However, at the beginning of the twenty-first century, Egypt must import food to feed its growing population. Oil and tourism have become Egypt's main sources of income.

During the 1970s, President Sadat began efforts to strengthen the private sector. Laws were passed to attract foreign banks to Egypt and to create favorable incentives for investment. This open-door policy brought with it success for some Egyptians. But the policies failed to address the needs of most of the population. In late 1976, in an attempt to make the country more attractive to foreign investors, the Sadat administration announced that it would end subsidies on several staple

foods. The Egyptian people responded to this announcement with nationwide rioting. The government abandoned the subsidy cuts at that time. However, many of these subsidies were reduced in the early 1990s.

Since the mid-1980s, the Egyptian government has made an effort to further restructure the economy by privatizing a wide range of companies. The policy of privatization has met with only limited success, as many of the companies Egypt has offered up for privatization are not attractive to investors. This is because the government mandate of the 1950s that assured a government job to every university graduate has left many government-owned companies overstaffed and inefficient. (In recent years, the Egyptian government has been largely ignoring this policy.) Fear of resulting layoffs has also slowed the privatization process.

In the 1980s, Egypt's economy suffered a decline when oil prices dropped. The early 1990s saw the country's oil industry get a boost from the Persian Gulf crisis, which closed off some sources of oil in other parts of the Middle East.

Internet service first became available in Egypt in 1993, with an estimated 2,000 users logging on that year. By March 2000, 440,000 Egyptians were using the Internet. Telecom Egypt, the government-owned company spearheading Internet modernization, is working to expand and upgrade the country's online capabilities. However, the cost of computers and Internet access is much higher than most Egyptians can afford.

The Mubarak government's decision to help the anti-Iraq coalition during the Gulf War had several economic benefits. International lenders canceled about one-third of Egypt's large foreign debt— roughly $20 billion—and some Arab states sent funds to support the country's war efforts. The lower foreign debt resulted in more international loans, which further eased Egypt's financial woes. Egypt receives about $2.5 billion in economic aid annually. Roughly two-thirds of this comes from the United States.

Egypt's economy saw steady growth through much of the 1990s. However, as Egypt moves into the twenty-first century, its economy faces many difficulties. Foreign investment began to slow in the late 1990s. Attacks on tourists by radical Islamic groups devastated the tourism industry in 1997 and 1998. The industry was making a dramatic recovery until it suffered a major setback in the wake of the September 11, 2001, terrorist attacks in the United States. That same year, the Egyptian stock market suffered a major slump. Official statistics have the country's unemployment rate at 9 percent. But independent economists estimate the percentage to be much higher—18 percent or greater. Egypt's economy continues to grow, yet it remains to be seen if it can grow at the rate required to feed and employ its 68 million citizens.

Agriculture

Although only 7 million acres (2.8 million hectares) of Egyptian territory are suitable for farming, a plot of land can produce crops up to three times a year because of the warm climate year-round. Agricultural production has stabilized since the building of the Aswan High Dam, which has eliminated the annual flooding of the Nile Valley. The flooding, while enriching the soil, also left the land unusable for a period each year. Major engineering projects in the southern and eastern regions of Egypt are designed to reclaim as much as 2 million acres (809,371 hectares) of land from the desert in the next decade, much of it for agricultural use.

All farmland in Egypt must be irrigated with water from the Nile,

Due to the dry climate, all Egyptian farms require **heavy irrigation** to remain productive.

since virtually no rain falls. Methods of irrigation in Egypt have changed little through the centuries. The most common way to water crops is by flood irrigation. Canals are dug east and west of the Nile, and water is raised into secondary canals by water screws or by pumps turned by animals. Occasionally, electric pumps are used. Once water has reached the secondary canals, fields are watered by unplugging a hole in a small earthen dike to permit the field to flood. The dike is then closed. Flood irrigation requires more manual labor than do more modern methods, such as spray or drip irrigation.

Land reform measures instituted after the 1952 Revolution broke up farms, and each farmer was given between 2 and 5 acres (.8 and 2 hectares) of land. The small size of the plots along with the use of flood irrigation make it difficult for Egyptian farmers to use mechanized equipment. Tractors and cultivators are rarely seen in Egyptian fields. Traditional farming practices require greater manual labor, which is plentiful in the overcrowded countryside along the Nile.

The absence of modern equipment also necessitates a higher

Harvesting dates

dependency on older forms of transportation, such as the camel or donkey. Consequently, part of the agricultural production must go to feed farm animals.

Cotton is Egypt's most important crop, and at least 70 percent of it is grown for export. The government stipulates that farmers use no more than one-third of their land for cotton production and that they devote an additional one-third to wheat. The policy seeks to encourage farmers to produce several crops, thereby decreasing Egypt's food imports.

Egypt also produces a wide range of vegetables and cereal crops—sugarcane, potatoes, millet, beans, rice, and onions. Sheep, goats, camels, and cattle are raised for meat, as well as for fresh milk and wool. Few farmers raise pigs, since Islamic law forbids the consumption of pork products. Villagers keep chickens for egg production. Water buffalo, horses, donkeys, and camels are kept for working the land. With a population that is increasing far faster than the rate at which new land is reclaimed for farming, however, the country can no longer meet its food requirements. As a result, Egypt must import from $2.5 to $3 billion worth of food from other countries each year.

Industry

Oil is Egypt's most valuable industrial product. In 1997 sale of petroleum products accounted for 44 percent of Egypt's total export earnings. The majority of the country's oil fields (70 percent) are located in and around the Gulf of Suez. Other areas of oil production are the Western and Eastern Deserts and the Sinai Peninsula. In addition to its value as an export product, oil provides 93 percent of the country's energy needs.

Oil rig

After oil, Egypt's most important industry is the manufacturing of textiles. Fabrics produced include cotton and fine woolens. Consumer goods—such as footwear, furniture, stoves, and tourist souvenirs—are manufactured in the cities. Outlying districts produce chemicals, cottonseed oil, and fertilizers. Other major industries include steel, aluminum, military equipment, and sugar refining.

Transportation

Egypt has an extensive railroad network that follows the pattern of settlement along the Nile River. The network includes 2,800 miles (4,506 km) of track, running from Alexandria to Aswan. Other lines run east to the Suez Canal and west to the Libyan border.

About 31,000 miles (50,000 km) of paved highways and 8,700 miles (14,000 km) of unpaved highways crisscross Egypt. Most are found in the Nile Valley and are built on a north-south axis. No superhighways exist, and traveling by automobile from Aswan north to Cairo can take a long time because of the number of animals on the road.

Construction of the first stage of a metro, or subway, system beneath Cairo began in 1982. It was completed in 1987 and included thirty-four stations and 2.6 miles (4.2 km) of track. Other sections have been added since then, with completion of the entire system slated for 2015. As many as one million passengers use the metro system each day.

Boats, the oldest form of transportation in Egypt, travel on the Nile and its tributaries. Ships ply up and down the 960 miles (1,545 km) of the Nile River in Egypt, and canals nearly double the amount of navigable waterways. Dhows and feluccas are traditional sailboats, but the majority of boats are motor-driven. In some places, animals walk along the shoreline, pulling flat barges through the water.

Trade and Tourism

While tourism earns Egypt the most money, export income also comes from other sources. The country's exports include raw cotton, cotton yarn and fabric, sandals, rice, vegetables, phosphates, manganese ore, mineral oils, petroleum, and crude oil. Egypt's major trading partners are the United States, Italy, Germany, France, and Britain. Egypt's imports include cereals, sugar, wood, pharmaceutical products, paper, iron, steel, and telecommunications equipment. Egypt's large population is a strain on its resources and requires the country to spend significantly more on imported goods than it earns

EGYPT'S TRAFFIC WOES

Traffic is a major problem in Egypt. More than two million vehicles clog the nation's roads. This is four times as many as the road system was designed to handle. The problem is compounded by the fact that many Egyptian drivers avoid traffic laws. Red lights are typically ignored, and cars often drive at night without their headlights on. The government has responded to the problem with stricter enforcement of traffic laws and by imposing stronger penalties for offenses. But these measures have not yet achieved the desired improvement in road safety.

through exported goods. Egypt's trade deficit for goods at the end of the twentieth century exceeded $10 billion.

Tourism is one of the largest sources of foreign revenue for the Egyptian economy, bringing in nearly $4 billion a year. The number of visitors to the country, however, often depends on international events. International terrorism increased during the 1980s, hurting Egypt's earnings from tourism. In addition, terrorist attacks on tourists by Islamic militant groups caused vacationers to stay away from Egypt in the late-1990s. In response, the Egyptian government imposed severe security measures, arresting and detaining hundreds of Islamic militants. These Islamic groups called a truce in 1999, and terrorist activity diminished. Egypt's tourism industry was rebounding until the September 11, 2001, attacks in the United States. At that time, concerns about foreign travel again devastated the travel and tourism industry worldwide.

Despite these difficulties, Egypt remains an important vacation spot. International cruise ships call at the port of Alexandria. Cairo's airport handles flights from all over the world and is a major transit

Thousands of tourists flock to the breathtaking **Temple of Abu Simbel** every year. The tourism trade is an important source of income for many Egyptians. For links to more information on traveling to Egypt, visit vgsbooks.com.

point to other parts of the Middle East and Africa. For many visitors, however, the most important attractions are found outside Cairo at the ancient pyramid sites of Giza and Saqqara and at Luxor. Luxor houses the temples of Ramses II and Queen Hatshepsut, as well as the tombs in the Valley of the Kings dating from about 1500 B.C.

◉ The Future

Egypt faces substantial challenges in the twenty-first century. The most difficult problems confronting the nation relate to overpopulation. Egypt's 68.3 million people place a tremendous burden on the land, on the country's resources, and on the government to satisfy basic needs. Although efforts are under way to curb the growth rate, the nation's population is still increasing faster than its agricultural resources are able to handle.

Another area of concern for Egyptian leaders is the economic vitality of the nation. In recognition of its supportive role in the Persian Gulf crisis, international creditors excused Egypt from paying a large part of its foreign debt. International banks have offered more aid in exchange for economic reforms, including a lowering of government subsidies on food and energy. Yet attempts at privatization have been hindered by the fact that many of the companies the government is trying to sell are inefficient and, thus, unattractive to investors.

Egypt's future depends on balancing economic progress and population growth. Egyptian leaders hope that the massive engineering projects that are under way to create additional arable land and habitation will address the needs of the population. Security measures have weakened militant Islamic opposition, but continued economic downturns, along with tensions arising out of the U.S.-led war on terrorism, could lead to destabilization.

3100 B.C.	King Menes unites Egypt and makes Memphis the capital.
CA. 2700 B.C.	The first pyramids—including those at Giza—are built.
2200–2050 B.C.	The First Intermediate Period begins. Clashes for power among families weaken pharaonic rule.
2050–1650 B.C.	The Middle Kingdom begins. Mentuhotep II reunifies Egypt and establishes his capital at Thebes.
1650–1550 B.C.	The Second Intermediate Period begins. Egypt is invaded and conquered by the technologically superior Hyksos.
1550 B.C.	The New Kingdom begins. Ahmoe I expels the Hyksos. Egypt develops a permanent army that employs Hyksos military technology.
1480–1460 B.C.	Thutmose III expands Egypt's territory to include Palestine and Syria. Thebes and Memphis become political and cultural hubs of the ancient world.
332 B.C.	Alexander the Great conquers Egypt and founds the city of Alexandria.
30 B.C.	The Roman Empire conquers Egypt.
31 B.C.	Roman general Octavian defeats Antony and Cleopatra at the Battle of Actium.
A.D. 639	Egypt is conquered by the Arab commander Amr ibn al-As. A new capital is established at al-Fustat. Islam and Arabic cultures are introduced to Egypt.
969	The Fatimid dynasty begins. The first Fatimid ruler, Jawhar al-Siqilli, founds a new city, al-Qahirah, or Cairo.
1171	Saladin overthrows the Fatimids and establishes the Ayyubid dynasty.
1250	The Mamluks end the Ayyubid dynasty and establish military rule. Egypt adds the areas that later became Syria, Turkey, and Cyprus to its holdings.
1517	The Ottoman Turks conquer Egypt.
1798	French forces, under the command of Napoleon Bonaparte, invade Egypt.
1801	British and Ottoman troops expel the French from Egypt.
1805	Muhammad Ali Pasha is appointed governor of Egypt.
1859	Construction of the Suez Canal begins.
1869	The Suez Canal is completed.
1882	The British occupy Egypt.
1919	Egyptians revolt against British rule.

1922 Great Britain declares Egypt an independent nation. Sultan
      Ahmad Fuad becomes King Fuad I.

1928 The Muslim Brotherhood is founded.

1948 Egypt and other Arab nations attack Israel and are defeated.

1952 A group of military officers overthrows King Farouk.

1953 Egypt is declared a republic.

1954 The Muslim Brotherhood is outlawed in Egypt.

1956 Egypt nationalizes the Suez Canal to fund construction of the Aswan High Dam.
      Britain, France, and Israel invade but do not gain control of the canal.

1958 Egypt and Syria unite to form the United Arab Republic.

1961 Syria withdraws from the United Arab Republic.

1967 Israel defeats Egypt, Syria, and Jordan in the Six-Day War. Nasser resigns as president.
      His resignation is not accepted.

1970 Nasser dies. Anwar el-Sadat becomes president.

1971 The Aswan High Dam is completed.

1973 Egypt and Syria attack Israel with no conclusive winner.

1977 A government announcement of measures to end food subsidies and other government
      programs sparks riots throughout Egypt. The measures are withdrawn.

1979 Egypt and Israel sign the Camp David Accords.

1981 Sadat is assassinated by members of an Islamic fundamentalist group. Hosni Mubarak
      succeeds him as president.

1988 Egyptian writer Naguib Mahfouz is awarded the Nobel Prize for Literature.

1991 Egypt joins the Gulf War coalition against Iraq, sending 30,000 troops to help protect
      Saudi Arabia.

1994 In several different events, Islamic extremists murder foreign tourists. The
      Egyptian government reacts by imprisoning large numbers of militant Muslims.

1997 Islamic extremists murder fifty-eight foreign tourists in Luxor, crippling the
      Egyptian tourism industry.

2001 High unemployment and a slumping stock market place Egypt's economy in
      turmoil. The Egyptian government condemns the September 11 terrorist
      attacks in the United States.

2002 Israeli incursions against Palestinian areas spark heated protests
      from the Egyptian public.

Country Name Arab Republic of Egypt

Area 386,660 square miles (1,001,445 sq. km)

Main Landforms Eastern Desert, Great Sand Sea, Jilf al-Kabir Plateau, Mount Catherine, Mount Sinai, Qattara Depression, Sinai Peninsula, Western Desert

Highest Point Mount Catherine, 8,652 feet (2,637 m) above sea level

Lowest Point Qattara Depression, 440 feet (134 m) below sea level

Major Rivers Nile River

Animals camels, crocodiles, Egyptian cobras, egrets, flamingos, gazelles, golden eagles, golden orioles, hippopotamuses, hoopoes, horned vipers, hyenas, jackals, jerboas, lammergeiers, lynx, moray eels, pelicans, scorpions, tiger sharks, wild boars

Capital City Cairo

Other Major Cities Alexandria, Aswan, Port Said, Suez

Official Language Arabic

Monetary Unit Egyptian pound. 100 piastres = 1 pound.

Egyptian Currency

Egypt's form of currency is the Egyptian pound. The pound is divided into 100 piastres. Egyptian paper currency is printed in Arabic on one side and in English on the other. Bills are not all the same size. The smaller the denomination, the smaller the physical size of the bill. The bills feature images of well-known Egyptian landmarks and symbols, such as the Temple at Abu Simbel, statues of Ramses II, and the mask of Tutankhamen, as well as pictures of famous mosques.

Egyptian coins duplicate the value of some of the Egyptian bills. Because of this duplication, many establishments in Egypt rarely have coins. In fact, the value of 25 piastres is so small that it is often difficult to find this amount in either coin or bill.

Fast Facts

Currency

The current flag of Egypt was adopted in 1984. It features three horizontal stripes of red, white, and black, with a golden eagle in the center. The golden eagle is the eagle of Saladin, the Ayyubid sultan who ruled Egypt and Syria in the 1100s. The red stripe symbolizes the period before the 1952 Revolution, when Egypt struggled for its independence. The white stripe symbolizes the revolution that brought an end to Egypt's monarchy and during which no blood was shed. The black stripe is symbolic of the end of the oppression Egypt suffered during British and Egyptian monarchic rule.

Egypt's national anthem was adopted in 1979. The anthem's lyrics are based on a famous speech by Mustafa Kamel, a leader of the Egyptian independence movement. The anthem's music was written by Sayed Darwish, one of the Arabic world's most popular composers.

"My Homeland"
CHORUS
My homeland, my homeland, my hallowed land,
Only to you is my due hearty love at command,
My homeland, my homeland, my hallowed land,
Only to you is my due hearty love at command.

Egypt! O mother of all lands,
Mother of the great ancient land,
My sacred wish and holy demand,
All should love, awe, and cherish thee,
Gracious is thy Nile to humanity,
No evil hand can harm or do you wrong,
So long as your free sons are strong,
My homeland, my homeland, my hallowed land,
Only to you is my due hearty love at command.

For a link to a site where you can listen to Egypt's national anthem, "My Homeland," go to vgsbooks.com.

INJI AFLATOUN (1924–1989) Inji Aflatoun was a painter, poet, and feminist. She is best known for her paintings of Egyptian peasant life. Despite being born into a wealthy family, she spent considerable time in the poor countryside, documenting the lives of Egypt's fellahin (farmers), particularly women. Her works have been displayed in many galleries and museums in Europe, the Middle East, and India.

CLEOPATRA VII (69–30 B.C.) Born in Alexandria, Cleopatra was the last of the Ptolemaic rulers and one of history's most famous women. In a life of romance and intrigue, she forged relationships with two Roman rulers—Julius Caesar and, later, Marc Antony—bearing children from both men. She used these relationships in a sometimes desperate struggle to keep Egypt free from Roman domination.

TAHA HUSSEIN (1889–1973) Taha Hussein, born in Maghagha in Upper Egypt, is considered the dean of Arabic literature. Losing his sight at the age of three, Hussein went on to enjoy a remarkable career. As the Egyptian Minister of Education in the 1950s, he was instrumental in bringing about free primary education for all Egyptians. Hussein's body of work includes scientific studies of Arabic, creative literary works, political articles, and translations.

UMM KULTHUM (1904–1975) Known as the Star of the East and Empress of Arab Song, Umm Kulthum is Egypt's most famous singer. Born in Tammay al-Zahayrah, a small village on the Nile Delta, she produced countless musical recordings and performed to sold-out audiences throughout the Arab world. Her clear and powerful voice is still heard daily on radios everywhere in the Middle East.

NAGUIB MAHFOUZ (b. 1911) Naguib Mahfouz, born in Cairo, is one the greatest writers of modern Arabic literature. Awarded the Nobel Prize for Literature in 1988, he has written more than thirty novels and numerous short stories. Some of Mahfouz's writings and opinions have been controversial. His 1959 novel *Children of Gebelaawi* was declared blasphemous to Islam and banned in Egypt.

MUHAMMAD HOSNI MUBARAK (b. 1928) Appointed vice president in 1975, Mubarak became president shortly after Anwar el-Sadat's death in 1981. He was reelected to the post in 1987, 1993, and 1999. Mubarak's administration has been marked by economic growth and strong measures to control Islamic fundamentalist groups. His administration also restored relations with Arab nations that opposed Egypt's peace agreement with Israel. Mubarak was born in Kafre al-Musailha in the Nile Delta.

GAMAL ABDEL NASSER (1918–1970) Gamal Abdel Nasser, born in Beni Morr in Upper Egypt, was co-leader (with General Muhammad

Naguib) of a group of revolutionaries who overthrew King Farouk in 1952. Elected president in 1956, his regime was marked by economic reforms, industrialization, and the building of the Aswan High Dam. Nasser died of a heart attack in 1970.

MUHAMMAD ALI PASHA (1769–1849) Often referred to as the father of modern Egypt, Muhammad Ali Pasha was of Macedonian descent but organized Egypt's government and military along European lines. During his reign from 1805 to 1848, he also modernized Egypt's agricultural system, expanding the amount of land under cultivation. He contributed to the industrial development of Egypt by setting up modern factories that produced textiles, glass, sugar, and other items.

NAWAL EL-SAADAWI (b. 1932) Born in Kafr Tahla, a small village outside of Cairo, Nawal el-Saadawi is a writer, doctor, and feminist. She has written many books and articles on the rights of Arab women, including *Woman at Point Zero* and *Woman and Sex*. Her feminist views and discussion of female sexuality are very controversial, as they are considered taboo subjects in Egypt's conservative Islamic culture.

ANWAR EL-SADAT (1918–1981) Vice president of Egypt under Nasser, Anwar el-Sadat gained the presidency upon Nasser's death. He instituted an open-door economic policy that encouraged foreign investment. Sadat's leadership is best known for two key events: the 1973 Yom Kippur War against Israel and the Camp David Accords with Israel in 1979. Sadat was assassinated by Egyptian Islamic militants in 1981. He was born in the village of Mit Abul Kom, in the Nile Delta.

OMAR SHARIF (b. 1932) Omar Sharif, born Michel Shalhoubi in Alexandria, is a world famous actor. He is best known for his roles in two classic films of the 1960s, *Lawrence of Arabia*, (for which he was nominated for an Academy Award) and *Doctor Zhivago*. Sharif has starred in dozens of English-language films since the 1950s, including *Funny Girl*, *The Fall of the Roman Empire*, and *Mackenna's Gold*. He is also a world-class bridge player.

DR. AHMED H. ZEWAIL (b. 1946) Dr. Zewail, born in Damanhur in the Nile Delta, was awarded the Nobel Prize in Chemistry in 1999 for his pioneering work in the field of femtochemistry—the use of ultrafast laser flashes to study chemical reactions. A femtosecond is 0.000000000000001 of a second—the speed at which many chemical reactions occur. The technology Dr. Zewail pioneered creates a slow-motion effect that allows scientists to actually capture pictures of chemical reactions as they take place.

ALEXANDRIA The ancient city founded byAlexander the Great lies on the Mediterranean coast and enjoys temperate coastal weather. The city features an array of cafés, mosques, churches, synagogues, and colonial architecture. The Bibliotheca Alexandrina (Alexandria Library) was completed in 2002. The catacombs of Kom al-Shoqafa, a Roman burial complex, date from A.D. 200 and are the largest of their kind yet discovered in Egypt. The Greco-Roman Museum features ancient sculptures, textiles, and mummies.

CAIRO Egypt's capital is Africa's largest city, with a history dating back more than one thousand years. Extremely crowded and bustling, Cairo offers the tourist an array of sights, sounds, and experiences. Central Cairo is home to the Egyptian Museum and the American University of Cairo. Islamic Cairo, in the eastern part of the city, has numerous mosques, palaces, and mausoleums dating back to the Middle Ages. Coptic Cairo is an isolated enclave within an ancient Roman fortress and features Christian churches and monasteries, as well as Jewish synagogues and ancient Roman architecture.

EGYPTIAN MUSEUM Opened in 1902, Cairo's Egyptian Museum is home to a huge display of exhibits, covering thousands of years of Egyptian history. The number of artifacts on display exceeds 120,000 and includes the Tutankhamen Galleries, home to the young king's fabulous treasures. The Royal Mummy Room has the remains of eleven ancient kings on display. The Akhenaton Room, dedicated to the king who worshiped the sun god Aten, features a display of ancient Middle Kingdom models that depict Egyptian life four thousand years ago, as well as exhibits of pharaonic technology.

LUXOR Luxor rests on the site of the ancient city of Thebes, Egypt's capital for most of the pharaonic period. It is home to the most impressive examples of ancient Egyptian architecture. These include the Valley of the Kings and Valley of the Queens, which feature more than a dozen temples and ruins. Across the Nile from these sites is the Temple of Luxor (featuring the Avenue of the Sphinxes—lined with seventy human-headed Sphinxes) and the massive Temple of Karnak.

THE PYRAMIDS AT GIZA Perhaps the world's most recognizable tourist attraction, the Great Pyramids at Giza are a breathtaking sight. The Great Pyramid of Khufu, the largest in Egypt, was completed around 2600 B.C. It is 478 feet high (146 m) and was built with an estimated 2.3 million limestone blocks. The Pyramid of Khafre (Khufu's son) is nearly as large as the Great Pyramid, standing 470 feet (143 m) high. Menkure's Pyramid is the smallest of the three, measuring 215 feet (65 m) high. Just as impressive as the pyramids themselves is the nearby Great Sphinx, the famous lion figure with a human face, and pharaonic headdress.

Arabic: the official language of Egypt and of Islam. Arabic is a Semitic tongue related to Hebrew and Aramaic.

caliph: a successor of the Muslim prophet Muhammad as secular and spiritual leader of Islam

delta: the clay, silt, sand, gravel or similar material at the mouth of a river that is deposited by running water, forming a triangular section of land

dowry: the money, goods, or property that a groom or his family pays to a bride's family

dynasty: a family that passes its ruling power from one generation to another

fellahin: Egyptian farmers

fundamentalism: a movement or attitude stressing strict and literal adherence to a basic set of principles. Egyptian Islamic fundamentalists believe the country's government should institute the principles of the Quran as the law of the land.

Islam: the religion of 94 percent of Egyptians, based on the Quran, as revealed to the prophet Muhammad

khamsin: a hot Egyptian wind blowing northward from the Sahara Desert in the south

muezzin: a Muslim crier who calls the hour of daily prayers

oasis: a fertile or green area in a desert or arid region

pasha: a person of high rank or office in the Ottoman hierarchy

pharaoh: a dynastic ruler of ancient Egypt

privatize: to change ownership or control of a business or industry from public to private. Egypt has privatized many of its businesses to attract foreign investment.

protectorate: a political unit dependent on a stronger power for its economic and territorial welfare

Sharia: the fundamental law of Islam. The Sharia consists of the Quran and the set of traditions that preserve the conduct and words of the prophet Muhammad. Egyptian fundamentalist Islamic organizations, such as the Muslim Brotherhood, want the Sharia to replace the country's current secular justice system.

Selected Bibliography

BBC (British Broadcasting Corporation) News Online. 2001.
Website: <http://news.bbc.co.uk/low/english/world/middle_east/>**(n.d.).**
The "World: Middle East" section of the BBC's website is an excellent resource for Egyptian and Middle Eastern news.

Central Intelligence Agency (CIA). 2001.
Website: <http://www.odci.gov/cia/publications/factbook/index.html>**(n.d.).**
The "World Factbook" section of the CIA's website contains basic information on Egypt's geography, people, economy, government, communications, transportation, military, and transnational issues.

Egypt State Information Service. 2001.
Website: <http://www.sis.gov.eg/front.htm>**(n.d.).**
The Egyptian Ministry of Information's official website contains links to Egyptian publications, images of the country, an Egyptian press review, information on the nation's politics, culture, history, tourism, and economy, and special feature sections on a variety of subjects.

The Europa World Yearbook 2000. London: Europa Publications Limited, 2000.
This annual publication includes statistics on everything from agriculture and tourism to education and population density. It also contains a detailed account of Egypt's history and current events, government, military, economy, social welfare, education, and a list of public holidays. Another survey explains details of the Egyptian government's structure, function, and constitution.

Library of Congress, Federal Research Division.
Website: <http://lcweb2.loc.gov/frd/cs/egtoc.html>**(n.d.).**
The section of the Library of Congress site titled "Egypt—A Country Study" presents an analysis of Egypt's political, economic, and social structure, with an emphasis on the inhabitants of the country.

Lonely Planet World Guide.
Website: <http://www.lonelyplanet.com/destinations/africa/egypt/>**(n.d.).**
The "Destination Egypt" section of this online guide contains information for travelers to Egypt, including a list of attractions and events, currency facts and traveling costs, and a brief article on Egyptian culture.

Population Reference Bureau. 2002.
Website: <http://www.prb.org/>**(n.d.).**
The annual statistics on this site provide a wealth of data on Egypt's population, birth and death rates, fertility rate, infant mortality rate, and other useful demographic information.

Statistical Abstract of the World. Detroit: Gale Research, 1997.
This is the source to turn to for worldwide economic and social data. You'll also find a comprehensive directory of each country's government, diplomatic representation, press, and trade organizations, and more.

Turner, Barry, ed. *The Statesman's Yearbook: The Politics, Cultures, and Economics of the World, 2001.* **New York: Macmillan Press, 2000.**
This source clearly and succinctly presents statistical information, as well as the latest details about Egypt's educational system, administration, defense, and energy and natural resources.

United Nations Statistics Division. 2001.
Website: <http://www.un.org/Depts/unsd/>(n.d.).
This UN site provides a wide range of statistics, including economic, environmental, social, and demographic data.

Weaver, Mary Anne. *A Portrait of Egypt: A Journey through the World of Militant Islam.* **New York: Farrar, Straus, and Giroux, 1999.**
Through extensive interviews with Islamic militants and leaders, as well as Egyptian military and government officials, the author explores the world of militant Islam in Egypt.

Barghusen, Joan. *Daily Life in Ancient and Modern Cairo.* **Minneapolis, MN: Runestone Press, 2001.**
This book for juvenile readers explores daily life in Cairo, from the time of its earliest settlement around 3000 B.C. through the dynasty of Saladin, the Ottoman Turk rule, and up to modern times.

Al-Bawaba: The Middle East Gateway.
Website: <http://www.albawaba.com/countries/index.ie.php3?country=egypt&lang=>
This online news site is an excellent source for the latest news of the Middle East. It provides separate sections for each Arab country, including Egypt, and features dozens of links to Middle Eastern travel, government, business, sports, arts, and entertainment sites.

Day, Nancy. *Your Travel Guide to Ancient Egypt.* **Minneapolis, MN: Runestone Press, 2001.**
This book for young readers takes a journey back in time in order to experience life in ancient Egypt, describing clothing, accommodations, foods, local customs, transportation, a few notable personalities, and more.

The Economist.com—Country Briefings.
Website: <http://www.economist.com/countries/>
This section of the *Economist's* website features fact sheets, news, economic data, economic forecasts, and explanations of the political forces and political structures of more than sixty countries, including Egypt. Also included are a map and flag of each country.

Heinrichs, Anne. *Egypt.* **New York: Children's Press, 1997.**
This book describes the geography, plants, animals, history, economy, language, religion, sports, culture, arts, and people of Egypt.

Mahfouz, Naguib. *Palace of Desire.* **New York: Anchor Books, 1991.**
This is an English translation of the second book of the Nobel Prize-winning author's Cairo Trilogy, originally published in Arabic in 1956. The trilogy follows the lives of the Abdal-Jawad family, a middle-class Cairene family. Through their experiences, Mahfouz chronicles the changes in Egyptian society in the first half of the twentieth century. This installment is set in the 1920s and focuses on a character named Kamal, a budding writer who is most likely modeled on Mahfouz himself.

———. *Palace Walk.* **New York: Anchor Books, 1990.**
This first book in the Cairo Trilogy introduces the engrossing saga of the Abdal-Jawad family in Cairo during Egypt's occupation by British forces in the early 1900s.

———. *Sugar Street.* **New York: Anchor Books, 1992.**
This final chronicle of the Cairo Trilogy finds the Abdal-Jawad clan dealing with rapid social changes in Egypt during the 1930s and with tremendous upheavals in family structure, in women's roles, in politics, and in the lives of the characters.

Middle East Times.
Website: <http://metimes.com/>
This website provides news and analysis of politics, sports, business, religion, and culture in the Middle East, including Egypt.

Pateman, Robert. *Egypt.* **Tarrytown, NY: Marshall Cavendish Corporation, 1999.**
This colorful volume for young readers discusses the geography, history, government, economy, and culture of Egypt.

Streissguth, Tom. *Egypt.* **Minneapolis, MN: Carolrhoda Books, Inc., 1999.**
This book for young readers is an introduction to Egypt, discussing the country's culture, language, people, animals, architecture, and land.

————. *Queen Cleopatra.* **Minneapolis, MN: Lerner Publications Company, 2000.**
Learn about the turbulent life of this famed Egyptian queen.

vgsbooks.com.
Website: **<http://www.vgsbooks.com>**
Visit vgsbooks.com, the homepage of the Visual Geography Series®. You can get linked to all sorts of useful on-line information, including geographical, historical, demographic, cultural, and economic websites. The vgsbooks.com site is a great resource for late-breaking news and statistics.

Captions for photos appearing on cover and chapter openers:

Cover: A Muslim man prays before the Pyramids at Giza.

pp. 4–5 The majestic Sphinx overlooks its domain at Giza.

pp. 8–9 Furrowed hills rise in the Sinai Desert.

pp. 20–21 Hieroglyphics, the ancient pictorial writing system of Egypt, adorn the walls of a tomb.

pp. 40–41 Two young Bedouin men gaze across the desert, as a camel waits patiently in the background.

pp. 48–49 A grocer and customer strike a bargain in a Cario market.

pp. 58–59 Egyptian pounds, the national currency, come in denominations of 10, 20, and 50.

Photo Acknowledgments
Cover: Photri/Richard Nowitz; © Photori, pp. 4–5, 14, 33 (bottom), 36; © PresentationMaps.com, pp. 6, 16; © TRIP/R. Cracknell, pp. 8–9; © Michele Burgess, pp. 10, 13 (top), 15, 23, 24, 42 (both), 45, 48–49, 53, 64–65, 68; © TRIP/B. North, p. 12, 44; © Joe McDonald/CORBIS, p. 13 (bottom); © TRIP/A. Ghazzal, p. 17; © Sandro Vannini/CORBIS, pp. 18–19; © Jay Ireland & Georgienne E. Bradley, pp. 20–21, 56; © Gianni Dagli Orti/CORBIS, p. 22; © TRIP/TRIP, pp. 26, 30, 34, 61 (top); © Musée du Louvre, Paris/SuperStock, p. 27; © Bettmann/CORBIS, pp. 28, 33 (top); © Hulton-Deutsch Collection/CORBIS, p. 31; © Ron Watts/CORBIS, p. 37; © AFP/CORBIS, pp. 38, 50; © Penny Tweedie/CORBIS, pp. 40–41; © Trip/A. Negm, pp. 46–47; © Dave Bartruff/CORBIS, p. 51; © TRIP/H. Rogers, pp. 52, 58–59, 61 (bottom), 62; © TRIP/E. James, p. 55; © Reuters NewMedia Inc./CORBIS, p. 57; © Robert Holmes/CORBIS, p. 63; Laura Westlund, p. 69